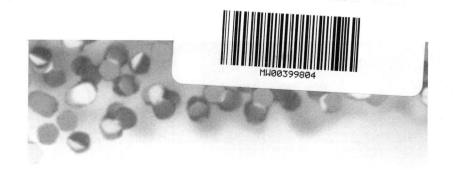

REFINED

finding JOY *in the midst of the* FIRE

CAROL BURTON MCLEOD

BRIDGE
LOGOS

Alachua, FL 32615 USA

ENDORSEMENTS

Refined is one book that could quite literally benefit anyone and everyone, for who among us has never known hardship and never asked the question, "Why, God?" Author Carol McLeod takes us on a journey into the very heart of God's goodness and offers a biblical response to the problem of evil. After reading this book, you may not have all the answers to your "Why?" questions, but you will better trust the One who does.

—Ann Tatlock,
   award-winning author of *Once Beyond A Time*

* * * * * *

I first heard Carol McLeod present the *Refined* message to a community of hurting, mourning, young men and women on a Mid-America college campus. The message didn't have the title it has now but its purpose and agenda was the same; finding joy in the midst of fire. In that moment of grief and pain, this message allowed everyone to breathe a bit more easily.

Life is messy and doesn't often make sense. *Refined* puts a language of hope to the process of spiritual growth through the fires of life. This book is humanly practical yet very spiritually inspiring.

I highly recommend this book to those who are faced with the daily woes of messy, unkempt lives. It teaches all of us that *"The Lord is good, a stronghold in the day of trouble, and He knows those who take refuge in Him."*

—Ossie Mills – Executive Director – Empowered21
   Vice President Strategic Initiatives –
   Oral Roberts University

* * * * * *

Whispered in a moment of frustration, or cried in the fire of crisis, we've all asked, "Why, God?" Carol Burton McLeod confronts this question head on in her book *Refined; Finding Joy in the Midst of the Fire.*

Carol presents solid biblical truths blended with personal experience and seasoned wisdom—insights gained from Carol's years of walking alongside others through life's heartaches. *Refined* leaves the reader with a desire *to* run to God and not away from Him in times of questioning.

—Marty Nystrom
   Writer of over 120 Worship songs,
   including "As The Deer"
   Author of *Don't Mess With Moses*
   Integrity Worship Leader

* * * * * *

Every one of us has asked, "Why is this happening to me?" *Refined* gives the answers to this age-old question in delicious, bite-sized pieces of truth and encouragement. Carol McLeod is masterful at building our faith in God's goodness by sharing Scripture and inspiring stories. Want faith? Read this book!

—Kathy Collard Miller, author of
   Never Ever Be the Same: A New You Starts Today

* * * * * *

If you have ever wondered, "Why, God?" then this book is for you. *"Refined"*, written by my friend and spiritual leader, Carol McLeod, is guided by the Word of God and presents hopeful answers to the questions that are birthed in the fires of life. Carol's passion for truth, for encouragement and for the Word literally leap from this book. No stranger to the fires of life herself, Carol has come through her trials with the fire-forged by-product of joy.

If you will take the time to read *Refined*, you will discover the goodness, the faithfulness, and the presence of God. If your life is a charred remnant of what it used to be due to a fire or two in life, you need the hope and the truth of this book. Carol doesn't sugarcoat her answers or give credence to platitudes, but she presents a solid biblical case for the presence and goodness of God even when life is at its hottest!"

You will find comfort in this book.

—Dr. Steve Greene – Executive Vice President
Charisma Media Group

* * * * * *

Carol's writing is firmly fastened to the words of God. She steers us past distraction and colorful lies toward the life that doesn't fade. *Refined* is pure Kingdom.

—Jared Anderson – Worship Leader and Song Writer
Founding member of Desperation Band
Writer of Worship Songs such as "Great I Am",
"Hear Us From Heaven" and "Promises"
(www.jaredanderson.com)

* * * * * *

Chock full of illustrative stories and scripture references, *Refined* addresses with clarity and maturity the big questions of God, the issues of good versus evil and the identity of the goodness of God himself in a world which sometimes seems out of control, both in our individual lives and corporately around the world. *Refined* is a refreshing, clear-headed, and practical look at how deeply we are loved, how God gives us only good gifts and sees us only through His lens of goodness. I couldn't stop reading. It will be a permanent addition to my library. Thank you, Carol.

—Amick Byram – CEO Oodles Entertainment
Two-time Grammy-nominated singer
and one-time Emmy-nominated singer
Amick sang the role of Moses in "The Prince of Egypt"
(www.amickbyram.com)

* * * * * *

Carol has written a book, *Refined*, that's a spiritual combination tool kit and first-aid kit.

Every page of *Refined* helps the reader understand that God uses trials to conform His children more into the image of Jesus Christ, no matter what it takes.

When you read Carol's writings, you just come to understand that not only is joy through tough times a viable option, but the only sane option for a Christ-follower.

Once again, Carol McLeod, in her latest book, *Refined*, drives home a signature theme of her world-view: joy can be found in any situation life may hand you!

—John Hull –
Global CEO of Crossroads Christian Communication
Host of 100 Huntley Street

DEDICATIONS

*This book is lovingly dedicated to two extraordinary women
who have found joy even in the intense heat
of the fires of life.*

To my college roommate and dearest friend—
Debby Matthews Edwards

*Whose husband, Pastor Steve Edwards, entered eternity
on April 30, 2005, following a tragic accident.*

*Debby has continuously lived with and shared the joy of the
Lord with the world around her.*

*Debby's commitment to the Word of God
has changed my life.*

Debby ... you are my hero!

*And to my daughter, Joy's, college roommate
and dearest friend –*
Cady Morgan Kendall Lewis

*Whose dear husband, Jordan, entered eternity on
March 20, 2014.*

*Cady courageously worshipped the Lord and fought on her
knees during Jordan's battle with cancer.*

*Although Jordan and Cady were only married for 9 months,
they have taught us all what true love looks like.*

Cady ... you are my hero!

Bridge-Logos

Alachua, Florida 32615 USA

Refined
by Carol McLeod

Copyright ©2015 Bridge-Logos, Inc.

Printed in the United States of America.

Library of Congress Catalog Card Number: 2015938692
International Standard Book Number 978-1-61036-144-6

04-27-15

CONTENTS

INTRODUCTION

"WHY?!!" AND OTHER DIFFICULT QUESTIONS

Why?

Why do Christians go through hard times? Why do the beloved children of a merciful, compassionate Father face unspeakable tragedies and heartbreaking circumstances?

Why? Why do children die young? Why do horrific accidents happen? Why do marriages break up, and why are people unfairly unemployed?

Why? Why do young men and women die in wars, and why do earthquakes violently disrupt the lives of kind, giving people?

Why do spouses have affairs ... and why do teen-agers text and drive ... and why does cancer target innocent, precious children?

Why do airplanes fly into buildings, and why do teenagers take guns to school to kill their classmates?

Why? The greatest theologians in every age at every juncture of history have struggled with the question of the unanswerable "Why?"

My prayer for this book and intent in writing it is that it will help Christians understand the purpose of the white-hot flames of life and why believers are allowed to go through destructive and anguished circumstances while serving an omniscient, omnipotent God.

We have all felt the extreme heat of life's circumstances and wondered, *"God! Where are You? Was this fire in Your plan for my life? Why must I go through this?"*

Although there may be no comforting answer to the

question of why, perhaps there are other questions that can be answered with the compassion of the Scriptures and the eternal loving-kindness of God. This book may not give a satisfactory answer to the question, "*Why?*", but it will endeavor to answer the other, just as difficult questions.

Does God send hard times into the life of a believer? Or, perhaps, does He simply allow hard times to enter our sphere of existence? Does God ever intervene in the gut-wrenching circumstances of our human lives?

And finally, the most telling and desperate question of all, "God . . . where are You?! Was this fire truly Your perfect will for my life?"

Before you decide to prematurely close the cover of this book, put it back on the bookshelf, and walk away, I can assure you that this book will not be a tragic diatribe, but it will be an encouraging and substantive thesis on finding joy when your world is falling apart.

The truth is, most of us avoid talking about tragic and undeserved pain because we mistakenly believe that if we talk about it, it will somehow happen to us or to someone whom we dearly love. Many Christians refuse to engage in this difficult conversation concerning calamity and hardship because of the spirit of fear that it confronts. Fear should never be a factor when discussing and then celebrating the ways and the wonder of our heavenly Father. This topic that I have framed with the word, "*Why?*" may actually be one of the very most important topics in all of Scripture.

The Word of God gives to the children of God the tools to comfort, encourage, pray for, and believe with people who are broken and disappointed with the circumstances and events of life. The world is filled with people who have been severely burned by the fires of life and who are desperately looking for answers.

This book is designed to be biblical, practical, helpful, and most of all, hopeful. Regardless of what you or your loved ones are facing today, know that you are not alone, that the Bible holds significant answers for you even in your pain, and that the God of the universe loves you!

Karl Barth, the great Swiss theologian, was perhaps the most important thinker of the twentieth century. His monumental work on church dogma filled volumes, and he is known to have preached over five hundred sermons in his adult life. One day a fledgling seminary student asked Barth, "What is the greatest theological truth of all?" Barth thought not an instant and replied, "Jesus loves me, this I know, for the Bible tells me so."

I pray that between the covers of this book, you will find the love of Christ and the truth of the Word of God.

CHAPTER 1
TRIAL BY FIRE

A TRIAL is any circumstance or event in life when one's instinctive, reflexive response is, *"Why, God?! Why do I have to go through this?"* There are certainly different levels of a *"Why God?! Why do I have to go through this?"* experience, but every level evokes that question with no expected auditory answer. Asking this question is often a frustrated attempt to garner the attention of the God of the universe. *"Why, God?! Why do I have to go through this?!"* is a desperate question born of desperate circumstances and desperately spoken from a desperate heart.

Different levels of *"Why, God?! Why do I have to go through this?!"* provide an interesting look at the ability of the human heart to deal with circumstantial pain and strife. Perhaps you have found yourself in one of these levels of human pain and fire.

FIRST-DEGREE BURNS

Backed up in bumper-to-bumper traffic, you are late for work on the day of a very important meeting that may determine your future with the company. *"Why, God?! Why do I have to go through this?!"*

You gain back the twenty-something pounds that you diligently lost last year before your high school reunion. *"Why, God?! Why do I have to go through this?!"*

It's your child's sixteenth birthday, and you were hoping for a pedicure together, a shopping spree, and dinner out to celebrate, but there is not enough money in the checking account. *"Why, God?! Why do I have to go through this?!"*

Although all of these issues bring frustration and certainly disappointment, they are minor irritations and barely cause a blister in the larger scope of life.

SECOND-DEGREE BURNS

Your husband lost his job after working thirty years for the same company. *"Why, God?! Why do I have to go through this?!"*

A child breaks an arm during the last play of the last game of the season. *"Why, God?! Why do I have to go through this?!"*

Your youngest child has just left for college, and you are forced to deal with the daily reality of an empty nest. *"Why, God?! Why do I have to go through this?!"*

Your twenty-year old dryer bites the dust, the transmission on the car dies, and you find out that you need a new roof . . . all in the same month. *"Why, God?! Why do I have to go through this?!"*

Your only daughter marries the wrong guy. *"Why, God?! Why do I have to go through this?!"*

This type of trauma is much deeper than the type incited by first-degree burns. The pain is longer lasting, and the cure is more difficult to find; however, in most cases, the flames of this type of fire are not life-altering.

THIRD-DEGREE BURNS

Your spouse of over a quarter of a century has just informed you that your marriage is over. *"Why, God?! Why do I have to go through this?!"*

The doctor has just informed you after a relentless battery of tests that you will never be able to have children. *"Why, God?! Why do I have to go through this?!"*

Being an only child, you have cared for your elderly parents by yourself for years. The doctor has just informed you that your beloved mother has Alzheimer's. *"Why, God?! Why do I have to go through this?!"*

After years of medical bills, pink slips, and trying to keep food on the table, your husband announces that you have no other option but to declare bankruptcy. *"Why, God?! Why do I have to go through this?!"*

Your only son has just announced that he no longer wants anything to do with you, your value system, or your family. He has boldly informed you that you will no longer be hearing from him or seeing him. *"Why, God?! Why do I have to go through this?!"*

Third-degree burns can cause your heart to break and your life to become paralyzed with no hope of healing ever again. If not treated immediately and with great care, third-degree burns can alter your life forever.

FOURTH-DEGREE BURNS

Your child is diagnosed with a fatal and fast-growing brain tumor. *"Why, God?! Why do I have to go through this?!"*

Your parents are killed in a horrific car accident. *"Why, God?! Why do I have to go through this?!"*

In the medical world, third-degree burns are categorized as the very worst type of burns and they can cause death. However, in the world of spiritual pain and human emotional suffering, there is a fourth type of life-burn. No one desires to experience this horrific type of scarring and blistering, but it is possible to experience fourth-degree burns and still be healed from the raw pain.

Who Is God?

Before you ever encounter another *"Why, God?! Why do I have to go through this?!"* moment, it is imperative that you set within yourself a correct definition of precisely who God is. Knowing who God is and understanding the characteristics that He eternally demonstrates is a theological issue that has the power to impact every single area of your mortal life. Knowing who God is, according to Scripture, will determine your thoughts, your desires, your prayer life, how you talk to people, the choices you make, how you worship, and how you process the difficult and devastating events of life. It is utterly and critically necessary that you know who God is, because man fell when he lost his right concept of God. If you do not embrace a correct definition of who God is, you may fall into depression, bitterness, and sin following the devastation of a trial. You may fall into losing hope, losing direction, and perhaps even losing faith if you don't know Him in all of His fullness and goodness.

The next time you find yourself in the direct path of a searing fire of life, you need to recognize who God is and glorify Him as such! If you refuse to recognize the character and goodness of God when the temperature of life is uncomfortably high, you are going to find yourself in a most dangerous spot in life.

For even though they knew God, they did not honor Him as God or give thanks, but they became futile in their speculations, and their foolish heart was darkened. Professing to be wise, they became fools, and exchanged the glory of the incorruptible God for an image in the form of corruptible man and of birds and four-footed animals and crawling creatures. Therefore God gave them over in the lusts of their hearts to impurity, so that their bodies would be dishonored among them. For they exchanged the truth of God for a lie, and worshiped and served the creature rather than the Creator, who is blessed forever. Amen. And just as they did not see fit to acknowledge God any longer, God gave them over to a depraved mind, to do those things which are not proper.—Romans 1:21–25, 28

In these verses from the Book of Romans, mankind became confused about what God was actually like. Humanity refused to honor God, refused to worship Him, and began to think that God was something that He was not. Although mankind falsely believed they were "know-it-alls," they were actually fools when they exchanged the glory of God and imagined that God was like them. These foolish specimens of humanity thought that God was no different from birds or cows or reptiles. These men and women, to whom the first chapter of Romans is referring, exchanged the truth of God for a lie. Mankind simply became confused about what God was like in truth. They did not know the character of God when it mattered the very most.

The fire will destroy your life and who God meant for you to be if you are unable or even refuse to focus on who God is. Knowing God, declaring God, and worshiping God while in the furnace of great affliction is what will transform your life into a trophy of pure gold living. If, the next time you find yourself saying, *"Why God?! Why do I have to go through this?!"* your second thought is about the goodness of God and you begin to worship Him in spite of the extreme heat of the fire, it may become your very finest hour.

"What comes into our minds when we think about God is the most important thing about us."—A. W. Tozer

CHAPTER 2
A FOUR-LETTER WORD

NICE TO MEET YOU, GOD!

The Lord also will be a stronghold for the oppressed, a stronghold in times of trouble; and those who know Your name will put their trust in You, for You, O Lord, have not forsaken those who seek You.—Psalm 9:9–10

If you know who God is, you will have confidence in Him even during the *"Why, God? Why do I have to go through this?!"* days of your life. If you do not know who God is, you will be unable to put your full trust and faith in Him. God's name is defined in the ancient Hebrew as *His character plus His reputation*. There are many, many people who, although they have cried out, *"Oh God!"* while going through a trial or tragedy in life, simply do not know His character or His reputation. Although they call on His name, they have no idea who He truly is.

The primary venue from which we are able to discern the nature and the name of God is the Bible. One must thoroughly study the Word of God and determine what the Bible says about our eternal Father. It is in the rich treasury of the Bible and in the expanse of its Holy Spirit–breathed pages that you will be introduced to the Eternal Divine known as "God."

GOD IS GOOD

Good and upright is the Lord: therefore He instructs sinners in the way.—Psalm 25:8

"Good" . . . isn't that a fairly boring adjective when used to describe God, the Creator of the universe? Coffee is good, and so is the weather. Church is good, and that Sunday dinner following church was especially good. Children can be good . . . parents are good . . . the stock market is rarely good, but ice cream is always good! Some crazy people falsely believe that Brussels sprouts are good, but those of us who are sane individuals know that chocolate is the very best good!

> *"Give thanks to the Lord of hosts, for the Lord is good, for His lovingkindness is everlasting."*—Jeremiah 33:11

Why does the Bible, the most complete and true Book of all time, merely describe God as the ever boring but completely useful "good"? God is the most creative genius in all of recorded eternity! God gloriously created giraffes, centipedes, canyons, and orchids. He designed Niagara Falls and the Sahara Desert. He engineered hyenas and diamonds. God is so much more than good! Holy Spirit . . . is that really the very best You could do when attempting to describe God in the pages of the Bible?!

> *The Lord is good, a stronghold in the day of trouble, and He knows those who take refuge in Him.*—Nahum 1:7

All other superlatives come after "good." If God is not good, then He is not powerful, nor is He faithful. If God is not good, then He could never be our Healer or our Provider. If God is not good— all the time— then it is impossible to trust Him or to pray to Him. God's goodness is the source from which His character and His reputation are birthed, and all other divine attributes are built upon the foundation of God's eternal and perpetual goodness.

> *I said to the Lord, "You are my Lord; I have no good besides You."*—Psalm 16:2

God is good totally . . . absolutely . . . and unconditionally. There is no bad in God, and there never will be anything less than good in Him. God longs to heal you and not to hurt you. God's plan for your life is to mend you and not to break you. God, who is the greatest good of all of eternity, desires His absolute best for all of your life every moment of your life. He longs for His goodness to seep into the crevices of every day of your ordinary but miraculous existence.

God is the greatest good that exists and is the Source of all lesser goods. Anything good that is experienced on Earth was birthed in God's heart and because of His eternal goodness. Creation was spoken into existence because God is good. Music was conceived in the good heart of Father God himself. The gift of family was given to humanity because God saw that it was not good that man should be alone.

INFINITELY, PERPETUALLY, BOUNDLESSLY, AND ALTOGETHER

The Psalmist was declaring resounding, irrefutable and eternal truth to all generations when he stated:

"I have no good besides You, [O Lord]."—Psalm 16:2

Everything good that we experience during life on Earth is conceived in the goodness of God the Father. There is nowhere else for goodness to possibly generate than from the Author and Creator of goodness himself, God.

Every good thing given and every perfect gift is from above, coming down from the Father.—James 1:17

There is nothing good that exists that has not directly had its conception in the heart of God, who is good all the time. God is the final standard of all that is good; everything that God is and does is worthy of our human approval. It is impossible for God to be *anything* if He is not that attribute completely. There is no bad in God . . . He is all good . . . all the time.

- *If God is, indeed, good, and He is, then He is infinitely, perpetually, boundlessly, and altogether good.*

- *If God is, indeed, merciful, and He is, then He is infinitely, perpetually, boundlessly, and altogether merciful.*

- *If God is, indeed, loving, and He is, then He is infinitely, perpetually, boundlessly, and altogether loving.*

- *If God is, indeed, kind, and He is, then He is infinitely, perpetually, boundlessly, and altogether kind.*

It is possible for a light to be bright but not "infinitely" bright, because one single light does not possess all the brightness that exists. It is possible for the tallest mountain to be tall but it is not "infinitely" tall, because one single mountain does not contain all the tallness that exists. But God is infinitely good, and there is no boundary around His goodness. Any molecule of goodness that has ever existed in all of creation has come from God.

God is perfectly good, and that is good news for you! Actually, it is great news for you! God never has a bad thought about you because He is infinitely good and there is no bad in Him! Think about it! God is never worried about you a single day your life! He thinks good thoughts about you every minute of every day!

> *For I know the thoughts that I think toward you, says the Lord, thoughts of peace and not of evil, to give you a future and a hope.*—Jeremiah 29:11 NKJV

God never changes; He is the same yesterday, today, and forever (see Hebrews 13:8). God's infinite goodness toward you never changes, nor does it ever diminish, nor does it ever waver. His goodness is always at full-throttle and full-steam ahead, because we serve a God who is enthusiastically good!

God's first recorded opinion was that light was good and that land was good. He declared in the first few hours of creation that trees, flowers, and asparagus were all good. God smiled as He spoke of the goodness of the sun, the moon, and the stars of every galaxy. God was unable to hold back His assessment as He stated that shrimp, humpbacked whales, and salmon were all good. God earnestly announced that mice, rhinoceroses, and cheetahs were all amazingly good! God's creation was good simply because He created it. God is unable to create anything that is not good, because He is the Source of all goodness.

Everything that God initiates or chooses to do is good, because all His actions are birthed in His goodness. God's mercy is His goodness to those in distress, and His grace is His goodness toward those who deserve to be punished. God's patience is His goodness to those who continue to sin time after time, and His healing power is His goodness to those who are sick. God's forgiveness is His goodness to those who have miserably failed or chosen poorly.

God's goodness is never exclusive and reaches toward every human heart. God's goodness is what makes life in the war zone of Planet Earth extraordinary. God is good in every way at every time. God is good . . . He does good . . . and He works all things together for good.

CHAPTER 3

GREAT = GOOD

HOW GREAT IS GOOD

How great is Your goodness, which You have stored up for those who fear You, which You have wrought for those who take refuge in You.—Psalm 31:19

The phrase "how great is Your goodness" communicates that the Psalmist understands that God's goodness is unable to be measured in human terms. If you were to live as long as Methuselah, you would be unable to tap in to all the goodness that God has stored up for your singular life. There is no measuring tape that is able to fit around the goodness of God, and there is no scale that is capable of weighing the immensity of His eternal goodness. There is no mathematical equation that is able to determine the amount of God's perpetual goodness.

When the word "*good*" or "*goodness*" is used in the Old Testament Scriptures, it can mean a variety of too-good-to-be-true attributes that are found in the nature of God himself. "*Goodness*" can be defined as "wisdom," "kindness," "wealth," "beauty," and "cheerfulness." "*Goodness*" is also determined to include "intelligence," "understanding," "property," "divine glory," and "welfare." And if that is not enough, "goodness" also means "happiness," "gladness," and, quite emphatically, the "best of everything"!

All of that and more, according to Psalm 31:19, is stored up, or set aside in a heavenly holding place for you. In the Hebrew, there are two types of holding places that are often referenced in the Bible. One type of holding place is hidden and inaccessible; the other type of holding place is one that is easily accessible. This life-changing verse, which was meant to introduce you to the goodness of God, says that God's goodness is a holding place that is easily and readily accessible. God's goodness is not locked away and hidden. God wants you to find His goodness! God's desire is that you would tap in to His goodness every day of your life! God is generous with His goodness and can't wait for you to benefit from all that He is and all that He has!

IT ALL STARTS WITH TRUST

The key that enables believers to splash in His goodness is called "trust." "How great is Your goodness which You have stored up *for those who trust you*" (emphasis mine). *Trust* is one of those words that can smack of religious righteousness if one does not fully understand the heart of God. In order to be lavished with His goodness, it is important to boil the religion out of the word *"trust"* and to make this five-letter word both personal and practical. Praying this simple prayer of surrender on a daily basis will enable you to fully trust in the goodness of God your Father:

"You are God . . . and I am not.
"I recognize You as the Answer to all of my questions
"and the Provider of all of my needs.
"You, God, are the Final Authority on everything.
"I don't have a better idea than You!
"You make me glad!"

The exuberant outpouring of God's goodness on your life begins with that bold declaration that is birthed in a heart of complete and unconditional trust! The words that are found in the beauty of Psalm 31 promise that God will bestow His goodness on those who simply trust in Him. *"Bestow"* is a lovely, yet archaic word, that embraces the actions of a good God toward His children who lovingly trust that He is who He has promised to be. The word *"bestow"* literally can be defined as "made and then given toward." God didn't create goodness to hold it away from you. God did not inform you of His goodness only to taunt you and hold it like a carrot in front of your nose. God did not pompously state that His goodness was for everyone else but not for you. God created His goodness to be given to you! God's goodness was made specifically for you! God has stored up His goodness, and when you trust in Him, He throws it enthusiastically toward your life!

Have you ever made or purchased a gift with a particular person in mind and then never given it to them? I am guilty of that so often! Even now, in my closet, there are several bags of gifts that were generously bought with a specific person or event in my heart. However, these perfectly chosen gifts lie languishing in my messy closet simply due to my laziness. And, if I were to be thoroughly honest, I will admit that I have completely forgotten for whom the extraordinary gifts were bought. God is never guilty of acting like this. God creates His goodness, He stores up His goodness, and when you decide to trust Him, He sends it extravagantly to you! Trusting God places you in the intended pathway of God's goodness for you.

And finally, this verse promises that everyone who takes refuge in the Lord will be the blessed recipients of God's perpetual and enthusiastic goodness. The phrase, "on those who take refuge in You," definitively means that when you find yourself in the brilliant habit of fleeing to God for protection during the storms of life, you will most certainly receive His goodness. When you run into His shelter, you have placed yourself in the position of receiving all the good that He has intended for you specifically to receive. If you determine to hide yourself in God while the storms of life are raging, you will discover in that safe place the goodness of God that has been stored up with you in mind!

When your world is falling apart, do you run toward God or away from God? Even strong believers are deceived by the lies of the enemy and make poor choices during difficult days of life. If you run toward food, or shopping, or spending, or worry when you are walking through a trial, you will find yourself unable to tap in to the lavish goodness of God. Conversely, however, if, when you find yourself between that infamous rock and a hard place, you determine in your heart that you are going to run toward God with all of your might, then His goodness will be chasing you down!

The next time that you find yourself in the intense heat of the fire of affliction, run toward God and not away from God. While the fire is raging and your life is endangered, do not blame God, but bless God! The foolish error that so many men and women of God make while walking through the flames of trials is that they choose to tap in to the false answers of our culture and not in to the wise answers of our God. Make the determined choice that the next time you don't know what to do, you will worship rather than panic. Make a willful decision that if you find yourself surrounded by the fires of tragedy, you will read the Word of God rather than choose to worry.

Continue to use the wisdom of God when your life is falling apart because God's goodness is always found in wisdom. If you are in a financial hot spot, do not stop tithing or paying your bills. If you are dealing with health issues, obey the orders of your doctor. And in addition to those wise choices, continue to worship and read the Word of God! God's goodness is on its way!

himself, at the end of his life, in charge of his dysfunctional brothers' destiny. When he looked at his aging brothers' faces, he was able to say:

> *"As for you, you meant evil against me, but God meant it for good in order to bring about this present result, to preserve many people alive."*—Genesis 50:20

Long-term Goodness

Finally, the fourth biblical and hopeful answer to this question that has echoed through the ages is that because God loves you, what He allows may not seem kind, but from His perspective, it can serve His kind intentions.

When my children were growing up, I made them eat their vegetables, forced them to practice the piano, and expected them to do their homework. They did not like my approach to parenting and often compared my narrow-minded ways to the parents of their friends, who allowed cookies for breakfast, video games all afternoon, and sleepovers on school nights. Those lenient parents made me look cruel, demanding, and no fun at all. However, in the long haul of life, my now-grown children have realized that although it did not seem like it at the time, I was the truly good parent.

It is impossible to judge God's ultimate goodness by our human standard of goodness. We are the fussy, immature children, and He is the eternally good Parent. It is imperative to remember that God's goodness is not just what makes us feel warm and happy. God's goodness does not make Him an endless dispenser of pleasure; He does not exist to indulge His children in what they mistakenly think they desire or deserve. God, in His wisdom and in His goodness, considers the long-term effects that may keep us from what we actually need and truly desire.

CHAPTER 5

TWO MEN AND ONE GOOD GOD

A GREATER GOOD

Because of the surpassing greatness of the revelations, for this reason, to keep me from exalting myself, there was given me a thorn in the flesh, a messenger of Satan to torment me—to keep me from exalting myself! Concerning this I implored the Lord three times that it might leave me. And He has said to me, "My grace is sufficient for you, for power is perfected in weakness." Most gladly, therefore, I will rather boast about my weaknesses, so that the power of Christ may dwell in me. Therefore I am well content with weaknesses, with insults, with distresses, with persecutions, with difficulties, for Christ's sake; for when I am weak, then I am strong.—2 Corinthians 12:7–10

Paul, the man who knew Christ in His fullness and in His power, identified the source of his "thorn in the flesh" in these familiar verses. Paul declared that his thorn in the flesh was a messenger of Satan. Although the greatest torment of Paul's life was sent from the devil himself, God used it to teach Paul a deeper dependency on the character and goodness of God. God is easily able to use the ploys of the enemy for a greater good and purpose in the lives of His children.

Paul begged God at least three times to take away the unknown "thorn in the flesh," but as far as we know, it was never removed from Paul's life. However, God used it to reveal His grace in Paul's weakness. Although Paul was not healed in the natural, he experienced the power of the living

Christ in his body and in his circumstances.

I firmly believe that God still heals today just like He did in the gospels and in the Book of Acts. When God heals a person physically, He is revealing His goodness and His will. However, always remember that the goodness of God is revealed in a multitude of ways, and healing is only one of those miraculous ways. Strength and power are God's goodness revealed in difficult situations and circumstances; patience and wisdom are also the strong evidence of God's goodness in a person's life.

OVERWHELMED BY GOODNESS

You are good and do good.—Psalm 119:68

Perhaps it is the rich life stories of ordinary men and women who experienced the goodness of God during days of great trial that speak the loudest. Allen Gardiner, who lived from 1794 to 1851, was such a man.

Allen was born to a Berkshire squire in England and had travel and adventure written into his DNA. His heroes were great men of the sea, and he determined to be a sailor before he was old enough to write his own name. When he was still a small boy, his mother found him sleeping on the floor one night. When she questioned him why he was not in his bed, he said that he was preparing to live the rough life of a sailor.

Allen entered the naval college at age fourteen and went to sea at age sixteen. He lived the raucous life of a sailor and traveled the world, even experiencing violence and war. The death of his friends and comrades deeply affected Gardiner, and he secretly bought a Bible and read it often while alone. Allen Gardiner came to Christ in China in 1820 after receiving the devastating news that his mother had died.

In 1821, he married and quickly had five children, but he

was greatly distressed by the death of his wife in 1834. Allen deeply felt the call of God on his life and traveled to South Africa with the intended purpose of winning the Zulu chief to Christ. The Zulu tribe was renowned for its savagery and love for war. Allen Gardiner's work with the Zulu people ushered in a time of peace between the warring tribes, and he did a great missionary work in a very short period of time.

When Gardiner returned to England, he married a woman half his age to mother his children, and the entire family returned to Africa to work with the Zulus. However, as they approached South Africa, his oldest daughter died. She was buried in South Africa, and the sorrow of losing her was enormous. He continued his work among the Zulu people until war broke out between the Dutch settlers and the Zulus. He was forced to take his family to South America away from the fighting. He wrote in his journal, ". . . disappointed but not cast down. Thankful for having been permitted to engage in any work that might contribute to the extension of the Redeemer's kingdom on earth."

Gardiner arrived in South America in June of 1838 and began, with his family, one of the greatest missionary journeys of the nineteenth century. They traveled through the Andes Mountains through perilous heights and on dangerous trails. He met with many of the aboriginal Indian tribes and presented the gospel to them, but the Roman Catholic Church asked him to leave the area.

Having been denied permission to do mission work in New Guinea, he and his family settled in the Falkland Islands for a year while endeavoring to reach the tribes there. After mission trips to Patagonia, Chile, Paraguay, Argentina, and Bolivia, Gardiner and a fellow missionary realized the only way to impact these nations was by basing the mission work from the deck of a ship.

He was unable to raise enough money to purchase the size of the ship that he desired, and so he settled on two very small launch boats. With seven men in his missionary party, they left Liverpool, England, in September 1850. Although they had never met one another prior to this voyage, they would never again part each other's company this side of Heaven. Having sailed the stormy waters of Tierra del Fuego, they were left alone at a place called Banner Cove as the ship departed the area. These men, who were intent on spreading the Kingdom of Christ, had come to evangelize the Fuegians.

They built a fence of thorns and put up a tent to protect their meager supplies, but the natives found ways to steal from the pure-hearted missionaries. The men, though heavyhearted, retreated to the launches, having lost most of their food supply. One of the launches went aground and was damaged beyond repair. Month after month passed with very little contact with the Fuegians, who were the very people that they had come to evangelize. Their food supplies were finally exhausted, and one by one the English missionaries began to die.

The diaries of Dr. Williams and Allen Gardiner reveal men who, though weakened in body, possessed strong and vibrant spirits and were assured of the goodness of the God whom they served. There was no blame or negativity among the dying men, but each ministered to and served one another with their last breaths. Twenty days after Gardiner's last journal entry, on September 6, 1851, the long-awaited help arrived—but it was too late.

"Ah, I am happy day and night, hour by hour. Asleep or awake, I am happy beyond words and the poor compass of language to tell. . . . As I day by day and night by night lie here, what a world, unknown to the world, do I live and have my thoughts and move my affections in!"

"God is indeed above my bed. . . . Let all my beloved ones at home rest assured that I was happy beyond expression the night I wrote these lines and would not have changed situations with any man living . . . that heaven, and love and Christ, which means one and the same divine thing, were in my heart."

"If I faint or die here, I beg of you, oh, Lord, that You would lift up others to send more workers to this great harvest field."

"I am overwhelmed with a sense of the goodness of God."

And finally, the last entry, written in the weakened yet powerful hand of Allen Gardiner:

"The young lions do lack and suffer hunger; but they who seek the Lord shall not be in want of any good thing."—Psalm 34:10

CHAPTER 6
WHAT EXACTLY IS GOD'S WILL?

BUILDING A LIFE PHILOSOPHY AND A FOUNDATION of God's character becomes the cornerstone of determining what God's will or plan is for an individual's life. Do we serve a God who is somewhere out there but not involved in our daily lives? Or is He intimately acquainted with all of our ways and working behind the scenes to knit situations and events for our highest good and His ultimate glory? Every believer must make that determination individually and must make it based upon the truth in the Word of God. Determining God's heart, character, and predisposed will based upon circumstantial evidence is the weakest of all human choices. The Word holds the indisputable answer of the revealed mystery of God's perfect and good will.

God's will, simply put, is what God desires or wants. God's will is found in His Word even in the darkest, hottest days of human existence. There is no other repository that holds the answer to the timeless question, *"What exactly is God's will?"*

ALL THINGS

> *In the same way the Spirit also helps our weakness; for we do not know how to pray as we should, but the Spirit Himself intercedes for us with groanings too deep for words.*—Romans 8:26

Jesus and the Holy Spirit knew that there would be times and situations in life when we, as God's dearly loved children, would face great human weakness. And so, because Jesus and the Holy Spirit realized that life would be devastatingly difficult, and that we, the children of God, would be exhaustingly weak, a message was sent through the Apostle Paul and straight into the heart of those feeble children. The Holy Spirit will always be with you to give you power and to give you the words to pray when you have no words in yourself. The Holy Spirit will pray through you and for you when you are too weak to pray on your own. If you can muster up the strength to cry out, "*Holy Spirit! Pray for me! Pray through me!*" it is in those desperate words that you will begin to tap in to His eternal power.

And He who searches the hearts knows what the mind of the Spirit is, because He intercedes for the saints according to the will of God.—Romans 8:27

The Holy Spirit realizes what is going on inside of human hearts, and He is also privy to what is inside the mind of God. The Holy Spirit is miraculously capable of bringing together the pain of our human hearts with the will of God the Father. He brings the pain of your heart together with the mind of the Spirit and then begins to pray for God's will to happen in your life! The Holy Spirit's chief job assignment is to know you, to know the will of the Father, and to pray for God's will to happen on Earth as it is in Heaven.

God's will for your life is always found in the Word of God. God's will for any individual is simply what God desires or what God wants. God's delightful, extraordinary, and miraculous will can be found clearly revealed between the pages of the Bible.

And we know that God causes all things to work together for good to those who love God, to those who are called according to His purpose.—Romans 8:28

In these very familiar words, penned by Paul and instigated by the Holy Spirit, we find the complete and unalterable will of God for anyone who loves Him. God's will for your life is to work every detail, every tragic event, and every compromising situation together for your highest good and for His glory. The Holy Spirit is praying that God's highest good will happen in your life because that is the focused will of God for you!

I used to mistakenly believe that Romans 8:28 meant in some cosmic way that God was going to rearrange the circumstances of my life so that they looked good. Somehow I thought that if something bad happened to me or one of my loved ones, certainly, because I loved Him, He would counteract the bad with something good or even better.

I hoped that if my car was wrecked, I would magically win the lottery and be able to buy a new car! Sounds good to me! After all . . . God works all things together for good, doesn't He?

I inaccurately supposed that if someone was mean to me, someone else, who was surely more important than that old meanie, would be sweet to me the very next day! After all . . . God works all things together for good, doesn't He?

I foolishly expected that if I had to buy a new dryer with this week's grocery money, somebody with a lot of money would take us out to dinner this week! After all . . . God works all things together for good, doesn't He?

I have come to understand that although those things may happen, in reality, those misplaced desires I conjure up in the fantasy of my mind are actually turning God into a fairy godmother. Those immature thoughts are making little of God's perpetual and enthusiastic goodness. The truth of Romans 8:28 is a deeper and more eternal miracle than a simple change of circumstances or events.

I had been reading this Scripture as meaning that each thing that came into my life would work individually for good, but that is not what is meant by the grammatical structure in the

Greek. The cumulative effect that God evokes does not take one thing at a time and work it for our good. This Scripture is not referencing each isolated event in your life as a single factor that God is able to change into something good. Romans 8:28 declares through the ages, *"God causes all things to work together for good."*

HOW TO . . .

Although I have never baked a cake from scratch, I know the process and procedure that it takes to make this domestic and culinary event happen in the practical sense. I watched my grandmother bake cakes from scratch during every year of my girlhood. My feisty little Irish grandmother would first lay all the items out on the counter that were needed in the old family recipe. I would see flour, baking powder, and raw eggs on her pink Formica countertop. In addition to those ingredients, she would add baking soda, vanilla extract, and cocoa powder in preparation for the mouthwatering final product.

As a young girl, watching my sweet five-foot-tall grandmother lay out food items that tasted perfectly awful by themselves, I was incredulous that anything delicious could come from such a sampling of bitter and tasteless ingredients.

"Gramma! Are you sure you have the correct ingredients? I want this cake to be the best one ever!"

"Carol," my wise grandmother would gently explain, "a remarkable miracle happens when all of these ingredients are mixed together and then the heat is turned on. The cake will taste absolutely delicious, I assure you. You will find this particular cake to be satisfying and irresistible, although judging by the individual ingredients, you would never believe that something could taste so incredibly good!"

My loving and insightful grandmother went on to explain

that life was a lot like baking a cake from scratch. When you look at what you have been given—trials, difficulties, tragedies, loneliness, and disappointments—you can't imagine building a good life on anything so horrible. When each of those events are tasted singularly, they are bitter, unappetizing, and even revolting. However, God is able to carefully mix the events of our lives, raise the temperature, and produce a masterpiece of a life!

IT'S ALL ABOUT JESUS!

The good that God is working from the painful and crushing events of your life is the good that He is working in you. God is placing His glory in your life and is leaving a deposit of all that He is inside of you. We have erroneously assumed that "good" is what replaces "bad" with circumstances, such as health, happiness, and pleasure. However, God defines "good" as what makes you and I more like Jesus.

> *For those whom He foreknew, He also predestined to become conformed to the image of His Son, so that He would be the firstborn among many brethren.*—Romans 8:29

God uses suffering to make human beings more like Jesus! God is well able to take what is perceived as bitter by itself and turn it into a revolutionary force in one's life that transforms anyone into possessing the character of Jesus. God delights in taking the things that have roared painfully through your life with the force of a hurricane and use those exact events to make you think and act and emote like Jesus. God's plan trumps the devastation of the enemy every single time. The enemy wants to destroy you with problems, challenges, and storms, but God intends to turn you into the representation of His Son, Jesus Christ. Jesus is your elder Brother, and it is time for you to start acting like Him! It is time for you to model your life after the life of your Big Brother! He came to be the "show and tell" of how to live well ... how to live powerfully ... and how to live in the goodness of God, the Father.

Oftentimes, God delivers His children out of suffering and tragedy, but He always protects us by shielding us with His goodness. I know a young bride whose husband died due to a rare form of cancer, and she is so grateful for the woman that she has become today, nearly two decades later. This is the testimony of her life: "*I wish that I still had my husband here with me, but I would never trade what I have learned and how I have grown through this experience in life. Losing my husband at an early age forced me to create an intimacy with the Lord that I never before imagined. How I wish that I could have learned and grown and known God like I do today and yet still have my husband by my side!*"

The testimony of this young widow captures my heart completely. I wish that I could have experienced the good that God brought through my pain without having to walk through the suffering and tragedy to achieve the good.

Everything that comes into your life is filtered through the Father's ultimate goodness. You can rest assured that nothing will touch your life that He does not allow and that He will not work for your good. Only a good, all-powerful God is able to take what is incredibly bad and miraculously turn it into something incredibly good. Every tragic event and disappointing experience that a believer goes through this side of Heaven should have one purpose and one purpose alone: to make each one of us more like Jesus.

If a greater good can take place by God allowing you to walk through something rather than being detoured around it, God goes for the greater good—to make you more like Jesus.

CHAPTER 7
THE "P" WORDS

LIFE AT ITS FINEST IS A PROCESS. It is a process of trials and blessings . . . of challenges and tests . . . of pain and delight. Life is a process of the *"Why, God?! Why do I have to go through this?"* days we all will experience.

God is using the process of life to turn you into something more beautiful than you could ever be without the process of life. God uses this process to turn a man or a woman into a productive member of the Kingdom of God. God needs you! His plan is to use you, and He is unable to use you when you stubbornly remain in the beginning stages of the process. God's process will always refine and define a child who is willing to be turned into someone usable for Christ and His Kingdom.

As twenty-first-century Western believers, we have embraced words such as *productive*, and *purpose*, and *prosperous*. However, all three of those "powerful" words are dependent upon God's "process" in the life of a Christian.

Often, the process that God takes one of His children through involves fire. Not one of us enjoys the fire, and all of us may scream and wiggle and complain in order to avoid the fires of life. However, even in the fire, God is refining, defining, and preparing each one of us for purpose in His unshakable Kingdom! There is a way to go through the fire and not even have the residue of smoke rest upon us. There is a way to be in the fire but not of the fire!

I must admit, I have experienced a fire or two in my lifetime, and often I have indeed come out smelling like smoke. After spending time in the "furnace of great affliction," often I come out as a charred remnant of my former self. But that is because when I was in the fire I was determined to have my own way and not God's way. I have painfully discovered that when you go through any fire in life guided by the principles found only in the Word of God, you will be able to encounter the hottest flames that life has to offer and still not smell like smoke!

But now, thus says the Lord, your Creator, O Jacob, and He who formed you, O Israel, "Do not fear, for I have redeemed you; I have called you by name; you are Mine! When you pass through the waters, I will be with you; and through the rivers, they will not overflow you. When you walk through the fire, you will not be scorched, nor will the flame burn you."—Isaiah 43:1–2

THE CLASH OF THE KINGDOMS

Once upon a time, when Nebuchadnezzar sat on the throne of Babylon, a true story is told of a group of young Jewish boys. These boys were from Israel and had been kidnapped by this nation of idol-worshipers. These pre-adolescent young men, children really, were chosen by King Nebuchadnezzar's right-hand man to be part of a young team of leaders whom they were going to brainwash into the ways and philosophies of Babylon. The goal of Babylon was to take the brightest and the best of the captives and then convert them to serve in the new kingdom in which they lived. Daniel, Hananiah, Mishael, and Azariah were never meant to be slaves or servants in Babylon, but they were in training to become great leaders in this foreign nation of Babylon.

Then the king ordered Ashpenaz, the chief of his officials, to bring in some of the sons of Israel, including some of the royal family and of the nobles, youths in whom was no defect, who were good-looking, showing intelligence in every branch of wisdom, endowed with understanding and discerning knowledge, and who had ability for serving in the king's court; and he ordered him to teach them the literature and language of the Chaldeans.—Daniel 1:3–4

So outstanding was this quartet of boys that their last names could have been Kennedy, Bush, or Clinton if they had lived in our own day and age. However, these boys were characterized by a virtue that many outstanding families in our generation lack. These boys were boys of valor and honor. They had purposed in their hearts and minds to serve their God regardless of the nation in which they lived.

The king appointed for them a daily ration from the king's choice food and from the wine which he drank, and appointed that they should be educated three years, at the end of which they were to enter the king's personal service.—Daniel 1:5

King Nebuchadnezzar, who was feared throughout the ancient world, was not known for being a benevolent ruler. The supreme leader of Babylon was cruel, intimidating, and all-powerful. However, because he had a prestigious role for these boys to play in his kingdom, he wanted them to be treated like royalty. There were to eat only royal food, drink only royal wine, and be educated as royal offspring. The Babylonian government was endeavoring to brainwash these Jewish kids and would spare absolutely no expense in doing so.

The king and his right-hand man wanted these young men to eat from a rich and tantalizing buffet that was lavish with choice wine and fattening, expensive food.

Now among them from the sons of Judah were Daniel, Hananiah, Mishael and Azariah. Then the

> *commander of the officials assigned new names to them; and to Daniel he assigned the name Belteshazzar, to Hananiah Shadrach, to Mishael Meshach and to Azariah Abed-nego.*—Daniel 1:6–7

King Nebuchadnezzar knew one solitary truth: If these boys were going to serve him wholeheartedly, he had to change their names. He wanted them to forget where they had come from and realign their identities as Babylonian through and through.

You, my friend, have an enemy who is cruel and unkind. One of the very first tactics that the enemy endeavors to accomplish while trying to brainwash a child of God is to change their identity. The enemy, in his dastardly and deceitful ways, tries to transform you into something that you were never intended to be. You have been made in the image of God, and your name is written on the palms of His nail-scarred hands! Your identity should always be extracted from God and not from who the enemy says you are.

Satan will try to change your name from "the righteousness of God in Christ" to "not good enough." The deceit and lies of the devil will endeavor to convince you that you are not "beloved by God" but are "rejected." He attempts to get you to falsely believe that you are not royalty, that you will never be enough. And, the lowest blow of all, is when that low-down, no-good, stinking liar tries to change your identity from "forgiven" to "guilty."

Never allow the devil to tell you who you are! As children of the Most High God, we obtain our identity from God's Word and from His opinion of us.

King Nebuchadnezzar may have changed the names of these three favorite sons, but he was unable to change their hearts. Daniel, Hananiah, Mishael, and Azariah were made for greatness in the Kingdom of God and not in the kingdom of Babylon. Even as mere boys, they had their priorities and their value systems set on the intangible, unshakable Kingdom of God!

DID YOU EVER HAVE TO MAKE UP YOUR MIND?

But Daniel made up his mind that he would not defile himself with the king's choice food or with the wine which he drank; so he sought permission from the commander of the officials that he might not defile himself.—Daniel 1:8

Daniel was the undoubted leader of the other three displaced, foreign boys, and he made up his mind that he would not defile himself with the king's choice food. Daniel made up his mind that although his feet were on foreign soil, he still served the God of Abraham, Isaac, and Jacob. Daniel made up his mind that the choicest of foods or the richest of wines could not be used as bait to brainwash him and his juvenile friends.

Daniel's resolve certainly changed history in this one verse from Scripture; because Daniel made up his mind, he paved the way for the other three boys to make a quality and wise decision, as well.

As believers traveling through this foreign world known as "life on Planet Earth," like Daniel, we must make up our minds not to be tempted, tantalized, or seduced by the smorgasbord of our culture. When the buffet of this world smells aromatically delicious, it is the resolve of a predetermined decision that will endow you with the strength to resist the compromise and the resolve to choose Christ and the principles upon which His Kingdom has been built.

These verses also reveal the importance of spending time

41

with people who know who they are in Christ and who have determined not to embrace compliance with the culture. Just one friend who refuses to give in to the world and all that it offers may be just the impetus that you need to walk away from an alliance with the enemy's opinion and offerings.

> *Now God granted Daniel favor and compassion in the sight of the commander of the officials, and the commander of the officials said to Daniel, "I am afraid of my lord the king, who has appointed your food and your drink; for why should he see your faces looking more haggard than the youths who are your own age? Then you would make me forfeit my head to the king." But Daniel said to the overseer whom the commander of the officials had appointed over Daniel, Hananiah, Mishael and Azariah, "Please test your servants for ten days, and let us be given some vegetables to eat and water to drink. Then let our appearance be observed in your presence and the appearance of the youths who are eating the king's choice food; and deal with your servants according to what you see."*—Daniel 1:9–12

The immovable and resolute Daniel was determined to live like a God-fearing young man in spite of the threat of death from his overseer. Daniel asked for a ten-day trial period of vegetables and water only to eat and drink. Daniel promised that at the end of ten days, the overseer could make a decision based upon what he saw in the faces and bodies of the young men.

PREPARING FOR FIRE

> *So he listened to them in this matter and tested them for ten days. At the end of ten days their appearance seemed better and they were fatter than all the youths*

who had been eating the king's choice food. So the overseer continued to withhold their choice food and the wine they were to drink, and kept giving them vegetables.—Daniel 1:13–16

What a remarkable principle presented in this historical account! What an amazing God we serve! When a child of God chooses to honor God in difficult and harsh circumstances, God will honor that child and give them favor even though it seems impossible. We truly do serve a God who is more than capable of making a way where there seems to be no way. Your daily decisions matter . . . they matter very, very much. How you deal with your culture matters . . . it matters very, very much. If you partake of the smorgasbord of compromise and pretense, there will be a high price to pay. However, when you choose God and His ways, although in the middle of the buffet of empty calories that the world offers, you will receive favor from the Kingdom of God.

As for these four youths, God gave them knowledge and intelligence in every branch of literature and wisdom; Daniel even understood all kinds of visions and dreams.—Daniel 1:17

I have often wondered if the choice that these four Hebrew boys were forced to make while drooling over cheesecake and lobster was the pretest for a certain lions' den and a particular fiery furnace. All four of these young men would be faced with something much more difficult than just saying, "No!" to burgers and fries with gravy. I wonder if the favor of God that they gained while refusing the temptations of their culture placed an inner strength in them that would not have been there without the first test.

If these four boys had devoured the royal buffet placed in front of them, we would never know their names. They would have faded into the background of Bible history like all of the other young men who were kidnapped at that time. They would have been one of the brainwashed generation who caved in to compromise at the most important crossroads that they would ever face. However, because they made up their minds and obeyed God during adverse conditions, He used all four of them to change history! Will you just be one of the many brainwashed Christians who continually partake of the buffet of the culture? Or will you make up your mind, refuse to be intimidated by fear or rejection, and allow the God of Daniel, Hananiah, Mishael, and Azariah to use you in your moment in history?

Every circumstance and situation that is faced in life will be used to strengthen your resolve and reaffirm your commitment and heart for the living God. God never wastes one experience that we face in life, but He uses every challenge, every test, and each heartache to build in His children the spiritual muscle of commitment.

CHAPTER 8

A HOT LITTLE STORY

Y EARS LATER, Daniel miraculously interpreted a dream
of King Nebuchadnezzar, after which the four Hebrew
young men were named as administrators in charge of
Babylon. These boys had gone from captives to chiefs in the
foreign nation because they had made up their minds not to
compromise their faith. The king even recognized the God
of the Hebrew children as the Lord of all.

*The king answered Daniel and said, "Surely your God
is a God of gods and a Lord of kings and a revealer
of mysteries, since you have been able to reveal this
mystery."*—Daniel 2:47

Although King Nebuchadnezzar momentarily recognized
Daniel's God as the Supreme Authority, he quickly developed
spiritual amnesia and decided to build a golden image over
ninety feet high. Everyone in the entire kingdom of Babylon
was expected to bow to this statue at the sound of the
Babylonian orchestra. If a person refused to bow to the
statue, made at the command of the king, the dissenter would
be immediately thrown into a blazing furnace and would be
instantly decimated.

These courageous young men who refused to partake of
the king's royal buffet, now refused to bow their knees to
the towering statue made of gold. When Nebuchadnezzar
heard of their rebellion, he entered into an angry rage and
ordered the young men to be brought into his presence.
The king wanted the whole truth from these boys, and so
he proceeded to ask them why they refused to bow at his
command. He reminded them, in no uncertain terms, of his

royal expectations and the punishment that would ensue if they continued to refuse to bow.

> *Shadrach, Meshach, and Abed-nego replied to the king, "O Nebuchadnezzar, we do not need to give you an answer concerning this matter. If it be so, our God whom we serve is able to deliver us from the furnace of blazing fire; and He will deliver us out of your hand, O king. But even if He does not, let it be known to you, O king, that we are not going to serve your gods or worship the golden image that you have set up."*—Daniel 3:16–18

These were the boys of the made-up minds! Intimidation was not a factor in whom they chose to worship, but they were filled with the faith that their God ruled from and sat on the only throne that really mattered in life. Shadrach, Meshach, and Abednego had no doubt about their shocking yet bold decision, and they knew that their God had the final say in the duration of their lives. These young men kept their gaze firmly locked on the unshakable Kingdom of God Almighty. They had purposed in their young hearts to walk by faith and not by sight. This immovable triumvirate was not afraid of the fire that King Nebuchadnezzar had threatened.

One of the principles from this scriptural account that echoes through the centuries is what came out of the mouths of Shadrach, Meshach, and Abednego when they were facing the fire. Although they knew that their choice would assuredly instigate a quick demise for them, they talked the language of faith. Doubt, despair, and discouragement were not allowed upon the lips of these young men.

> *"Our God whom we serve is able to deliver us from the furnace of blazing fire; and He will deliver us out of your hand, O king. But even if He does not, let it*

be known to you, O king, that we are not going to serve your gods or worship the golden image that you have set up."

The threat of an undeserved yet ferocious fire in life will undoubtedly reveal in a unique way the depth and richness of your faith. If, when realizing the hazard of an out-of-control blaze, you speak forth doubt, negativity, and fear, it reveals that you are likely walking by sight and not by faith. The vocabulary that defines men and women of resolve always echoes the hearts and mouths that were exemplified by Shadrach, Meshach, and Abednego.

Beloved, do not be surprised at the fiery ordeal among you, which comes upon you for your testing, as though some strange thing were happening to you; but to the degree that you share the sufferings of Christ, keep on rejoicing, so that also at the revelation of His glory you may rejoice with exultation.—1 Peter 4:12–13

If you have found yourself facing a roaring inferno, learn from the example of the three Hebrew boys and take the advice of the Apostle Peter, *"Do not be surprised but keep on rejoicing!"* The example of a trio of teens and the wisdom of a man who walked on water ricochet down through the centuries into your hot spot: *"Do not be surprised but keep on rejoicing!"*

Don't be shocked when an enemy culture turns up the heat and threatens your very existence. Don't be astonished when the wildfire of enemy warfare is searing and relentless, but instead, *"Rejoice with exultation!"*

If a fire looms on the horizon of your life, begin to worship and celebrate the goodness of God. As a blistering blaze comes into your life, refuse fear and instigate worship.

We are not a people who fear the fire, but we are a people who rejoice in spite of the fire!

IN SPITE OF THE HEAT

One of the divine secrets that the Bible teaches is the principle of standing in faith and holding up the shield of faith whenever a believer encounters a fiery experience. Sometimes this can be a nebulous principle to ascertain what it actually means to "stand in faith" or "hold up the shield of faith," but let's endeavor to make it practical together.

> *In addition to all, taking up the shield of faith with which you will be able to extinguish all the flaming arrows of the evil one.*—Ephesians 6:16

This Scripture clearly resounds with incredible news for you as you face the enemy's fire: *"You have your faith to get you through the fires of life!"* This is only one of the many reasons why faith is so valuable to believers as we travel through the war zone of Earth. Our faith is a weapon of utmost importance, and when used as a shield, it is miraculously and powerfully able to extinguish any fire that is set by the evil one. When the Holy Spirit spoke through Paul to write these words that would resonate through the centuries, He clearly stated the origin of the flaming arrows that regularly attack believers. All flaming arrows are aimed at your life and then thrown your way by the evil one.

Knowing that the shield of faith is indispensable when it comes to fighting fires, what exactly is it? One of the most important actions taken to signify that our shield of faith is in place is found in the words that we speak when we face a fire. It is easy when life is pleasant and simple to speak words of thanksgiving, worship, and faith, but it is infinitely more difficult to do so when life is red-hot and searing. When you find yourself facing fire or in an uncomfortable position in life, will you still defy the fire with the words of faith that you speak?

I have often coached my children about how to act and what to say in potentially difficult situations in life. When they were toddlers, I would remind them not to talk to strangers, to be polite to their grandparents, and to say "please" and "thank you" when given a gift. When my children were in elementary school, I would remind them often that they were not allowed to say words like *"stupid," "dumb,"* or *"shut up."* When my five children reached the teenage years, we would rehearse over and over again how to respond if someone offered them drugs or alcohol or if they found themselves in an uncomfortable situation with someone of the opposite sex. It is vital to plan ahead of time how to respond and what to say when the fires of life are threatening.

Whenever I face a trial or discover that a flaming arrow of the enemy has been aimed in my direction, I immediately go to the Word of God and ask the Holy Spirit to give me a specific Scripture for the situation that I am facing. I then take this Scripture and write it out, memorize it, and declare it and pray it!

For instance, if in front of you lies a gargantuan task that you are unable to tackle or complete in your own strength:

I can do all things through [Christ] who strengthens me.—Philippians 4:13

Or perhaps you are facing a great evil or a great wrong done toward you:

No weapon that is formed against you will prosper; and every tongue that accuses you in judgment you will condemn. This is the heritage of the servants of the Lord, and their vindication is from Me," declares the Lord.—Isaiah 54:17

Or maybe you have traveled such a difficult road that you have forgotten the many, many blessings and promises of God:

Bless the Lord, O my soul, and all that is within me, bless His holy name. Bless the LORD, O my soul, and forget none of His benefits; who pardons all your iniquities, who heals all your diseases; who redeems your life from the pit, who crowns you with lovingkindness and compassion; who satisfies your years with good things, so that your youth is renewed like the eagle.—Psalm 103:1–5

Scripture has been given to us not merely to read like the daily newspaper, not merely to study like an academic textbook, but it has been given to us as a powerful, protective covering and heat-resistant shield as the flames of life dance around us.

Shadrach, Meshach, and Abednego spoke words of faith when in the very hottest situation of their young lives. Holding up your shield of faith is choosing to worship and then declaring the Word of God as a vibrant and cooling fountain that is capable of quenching the fiery darts or lowering the temperature of the fiery furnace. If the fire continues to rage and fear enters your heart, worship louder!

And without faith it is impossible to please Him, for he who comes to God must believe that He is and that He is a rewarder of those who seek Him.—Hebrews 11:6

There is no doubt but that Shadrach, Meshach, and Abednego were pleasing to the Lord at this moment in their young lives. Their faith was active and courageous, and they exhibited an unshakable belief in the King of all kings. So it is with you and me. When we come to God in the moment that the fire is at its most intense, we must believe in His power, and this will bring pleasure to our great God! As we, like the three Hebrew boys, exhibit an unshakable faith and declare God's power over our fire, God will surely reward us with blessings and protection beyond measure.

Perhaps the next time that you face a fire, rather than wailing and whining and worrying, you might choose to pray this prayer:

"God, I believe You are well able to protect me, and I believe that You always reward those who seek You. Father, I worship You in this moment, knowing that You, and not the fire, will have the final say in my life."

THE HOT LITTLE STORY GETS EXPONENTIALLY HOTTER

These extraordinary young men did not walk by what they saw in the natural, they were not governed by the whims of their culture, and they were not afraid of losing their prestigious jobs. Their entire lives were on the line, and yet they chose to stand in faith and keep their eyes focused on the invisible yet all-powerful God!

For we walk by faith, not by sight.—2 Corinthians 5:7

It would be ridiculous to walk through life with your eyes tightly closed, wouldn't it? Can you even imagine the damage that you would do and the injuries that you would sustain? If a person chose to walk through life with his or her eyes closed, this foolish person would bump into walls, fall down stairs, and suffer from repeated and numerous bruises. As Christians, that is exactly what we are doing when we walk by sight and not by faith. If you choose only to see what you see, you have put on a spiritual blindfold and will go through life banging into situations, falling into Satan's traps, and sustain repeated battle scars. Open up your eyes and look at Christ and His promises! As believers, we do not travel through life the same way that unbelievers choose to travel. We must view every life event, every difficult person, every fiery furnace through our faith and through God's authority. Unbelievers only see what they see; believers see what God sees!

Then Nebuchadnezzar was filled with wrath, and his facial expression was altered toward Shadrach, Meshach and Abednego. He answered by giving orders to heat the furnace seven times more than it was usually heated.—Daniel 3:19

The pompous, controlling Nebuchadnezzar, because he was filled with emotion and not with faith, was a victim of spiritual amnesia. He neglected to remember that he had recognized the God of these Hebrew young men as the Lord of all lords. And so, because Nebuchadnezzar was unable to wisely respond to the convictions of Shadrach, Meshach, and Abednego, he ordered the already searing fire to be heated seven times hotter than it already was. The raging anger of the maniac king was declaring, "Get this fire as hot as possible!"

A normal log fire burns at an average of 450 degrees Fahrenheit; the fire of this angry king's making was raging at nearly 3,150 degrees when the Hebrew boys were thrown into it.

When you determine to take a stand in faith and refuse to give in or give up when the fires of life are blazing, you will make your enemy very, very angry indeed. Things may heat up for you before you see the hand of God move on your behalf. But never assess the power or goodness of your God by the heat of your fire. The time that passes between the utterance of your prayer and when His answer is delivered is called "the testing of your faith." Most people tend to give up when they pray and then nothing happens. Most people become negative, fearful, or bitter when the temperature of their fire is multiplied by seven. However, it is vital that you remember that the goodness and power of your God is unaffected by the temperature of the fire.

WARRIORS OR WIMPS

He commanded certain valiant warriors who were in his army to tie up Shadrach, Meshach and Abednego in order to cast them into the furnace of blazing fire.—Daniel 3:20

The great and powerful king, whose reputation cast a shadow of fear across his entire kingdom, chose his strongest and brawniest guards to tie up the three young men. In the natural, this seemed like an authoritative move on the part of the carnal king; however, what he was soon to discover is that even Satan's best is no match for the people of God. When the Holy Spirit saw King Nebuchadnezzar's valiant warriors who were most likely muscular and drooling, His first thought was, "What a bunch of wimps!"

Shadrach, Meshach, and Abednego were surrounded by circumstantial evidence that was intimidating and horrendous. In the natural, they saw a fire that had been heated seven times hotter, a ruler out of control with anger, and a gang of hellacious bouncers headed right for them! But this band of three brothers of the faith was not focused on their circumstances or on what they saw in the natural. I believe that these courageous, faithful men looked toward the fire and saw Someone waiting for them there! When a believer, at any moment in history, chooses to walk and talk by faith, it miraculously changes what he or she is able to see. Rather than seeing fire, brawn, or anger, these boys saw Jesus!

What do you see? Do you only see the fire that is roaring and inescapable? Or do you see Jesus in the fire? Jesus is in the fire waiting for you, just like He was waiting for Shadrach, Meshach, and Abednego.

Then these men were tied up in their trousers, their coats, their caps and their other clothes, and were cast into the midst of the furnace of blazing fire. For this reason, because the king's command was urgent and the furnace had been made extremely hot, the flame of the fire slew those men who carried up Shadrach, Meshach and Abed-nego.—Daniel 3:21–22

The valiant warriors of the kingdom of Babylon were immediately massacred by the horrific heat that was not able to even faze the faith-filled men of God!

THE FOURTH MAN

But these three men, Shadrach, Meshach and Abednego, fell into the midst of the furnace of blazing fire still tied up.—Daniel 3:23

When the three Hebrew men first encountered the fire, Scripture recounts that they were still tied up in their clothes. Their hands were tied to their sides, and their legs were tied together so that they were unable to escape.

Then Nebuchadnezzar the king was astounded and stood up in haste; he said to his high officials, "Was it not three men we cast bound into the midst of the fire?" They replied to the king, "Certainly, O king." He said, "Look! I see four men loosed and walking about in the midst of the fire without harm, and the appearance of the fourth is like a son of the gods!"—Daniel 3:24–25

The powerful and controlling Nebuchadnezzar was incredulous! What he saw in the fiery furnace was causing him to experience dry-mouthed fear and heart-pounding panic. The greatest earthly king who had ever lived saw not three men, but *four* men in the furnace that had been heated seven times hotter than usual. He also noticed a peculiar and troubling detail concerning these men: They were no longer bound and tied up, but they were loosed and walking about!

Shadrach, Meshach, and Abednego were having the worship service of their life! While in a fire that had slayed the wimps of the kingdom of darkness, these three courageous, faith-filled men were dancing with Jesus! They were not burning alive, but they were in the presence of the greatest King who would ever live at any time in history.

You, my friend, are never alone in the furnace of great affliction. While the flames of your circumstances rage and the heat of the battle intensifies . . . you are not alone. Will you be brave and faithful enough to worship in the fire? If you can make the courageous choice that was modeled by Shadrach, Meshach, and Abednego, Jesus will show up in your fire! The fire may just be the life experience that will loose you from the things of this world that have been used to bind you. Praise is the key, for every believer at every moment in history to get through the fire and not even smell like smoke.

NOT EVEN THE SMELL OF SMOKE

> *Then Nebuchadnezzar came near to the door of the furnace of blazing fire; he responded and said, "Shadrach, Meshach and Abednego, come out, you servants of the Most High God, and come here!" Then Shadrach, Meshach and Abednego came out of the midst of the fire.*—Daniel 3:26

King Nebuchadnezzar not only called them by their names, but he recognized these extraordinary young men as servants of the Most High God. No longer were they his personal satraps or administrators, but he acknowledged that they served a Ruler much higher and more powerful than the king of Babylon. The faith of Shadrach, Meshach, and Abed-nego established their definitive position in the Kingdom of God.

When a child of God determines to talk in faith and to worship rather than whine, even the enemy will recognize whom you serve.

> *The satraps, the prefects, the governors and the king's high officials gathered around and saw in regard to these men that the fire had no effect on the bodies of these men nor was the hair of their head singed, nor were their trousers damaged, nor had the smell of fire even come upon them.*—Daniel 3:27

This verse clearly states what damage the fire inflicted upon the boys of the Hebrew nation: ABSOLUTELY NONE! There were neither short-term nor long-term effects that impacted these young men of faith and worship. Their clothes were in perfect condition, their bodies were not burned or blistered, their hair was not singed or charred, and these boys didn't even smell like smoke!

> *By faith . . . quenched the power of fire . . . men of whom the world was not worthy.*—Hebrews 11:33–34, 38

The writer of the Book of Hebrews in the New Testament was clearly referring to Shadrach, Meshach, and Abednego nearly seven hundred years after their encounter with not only a fiery furnace, but also with an angry king and his behemoth bodyguards. Paul, who almost certainly wrote the Book of Hebrews, pointed out an interesting concept concerning their defiant faith. Paul states that their faith did not quench the fire, but it quenched the *power* of the fire. Fires are a part of the challenges of life on Earth away from the safety of Heaven; however, faith in the life of a believer is able to dismantle the heat and destructive properties of every fire encountered.

When the enemy raises the temperature of the fire, your faith turns it into a cooling and refreshing experience.

> *But now, thus says the Lord, your Creator, O Jacob, and He who formed you, O Israel, "Do not fear, for I have redeemed you; I have called you by name; you are Mine! When you pass through the waters, I will be with you; and through the rivers, they will not overflow you. When you walk through the fire, you will not be scorched."*—Isaiah 43:1–2

The promise of God to protect a believer in the middle of roaring and searing flames is guaranteed through the words of the Holy Spirit through the prophet Isaiah: *"When you walk through the fire, you will not be scorched."* It's a promise of God that you will not even smell like smoke, no matter what kind of heat you may encounter. It is imperative that you determine to talk in faith when confronting a fire and stand firm in what God has promised. Never doubt in the roar and heat of the flames what God promised in the cool of temperate conditions.

GROW UP!

> *Nebuchadnezzar responded and said, "Blessed be the God of Shadrach, Meshach and Abednego, who has sent His angel and delivered His servants who put their trust in Him, violating the king's command, and yielded up their bodies so as not to serve or worship any god except their own God."*—Daniel 3:28

Who in the world is this benevolent and understanding king, and what did he do with his evil alter ego?! The ambitious and feared Nebuchadnezzar had a moment of spiritual clarity and applauded the young men for their strong faith and their choice to worship their own God. The boys who had been kidnapped from the Hebrew nation became well-respected and mature men through the process of the fire.

A fire has the positive capability of maturing your faith and your resolve if you are able to face it with faith and worship. The Holy Spirit may have been referring to these boys who became men when He wrote these words through the Apostle Paul:

Be on the alert, stand firm in the faith, act like men, be strong.—1 Corinthians 16:13

Those four commands, found nestled in the words of 1 Corinthians 16:13, remind every believer in this generation how to respond when facing a fire: *"Be on the alert . . . stand firm in the faith . . . act like men . . . be strong."*

THE REST OF THE STORY

"Therefore I make a decree that any people, nation or tongue that speaks anything offensive against the God of Shadrach, Meshach and Abednego shall be torn limb from limb and their houses reduced to a rubbish heap, inasmuch as there is no other god who is able to deliver in this way." Then the king caused Shadrach, Meshach and Abed-nego to prosper in the province of Babylon.—Daniel 3:29–30

Your fire may not even be about you, but it may be about your culture recognizing the God whom you serve. As a man or woman of faith at this moment in history, the Holy Spirit may be calling your name to stand in faith and to worship during the most intense and blistering flames imaginable. There is a dying world that needs to observe how one man or one woman reacts when surrounded by an unfair, undeserved, and relentless blaze. The world will recognize your God when you choose to stand in faith and to worship.

CHAPTER 9

THE GREATER WORK

A SILVERSMITH holds a piece of silver in his hand and carefully studies it from all angles. When his thorough assessment of the piece of silver is complete, he then holds it carefully over the prepared fire and allows the silver to be exposed to the heat of the fire. The silversmith will eventually hold this precious and observed piece of metal over the hottest part of the blaze that is in the very middle of the fire. The reason that the silversmith desires this valuable piece of silver to spend time over the fiercest aspect of the fire is in order to rid the silver of all of its impurities.

The silversmith never leaves the fire or the silver; he refuses to allow the silver to encounter the flames without the protection of his watchful and expert vision. If the silver was left even an instant too long over the intense heat of the flames, it would be destroyed. The silversmith knows that his chosen piece of silver is fully refined when he can see his reflection in the silver. According to the expert insight and experience of the silversmith, there are two purposes for the silver to be refined by the roaring temperature of the fire. The first purpose is to remove any existing impurities, and the second purpose is to see the reflection of the silversmith. The silversmith intimately and uniquely understands that the silver is being prepared for a greater work.

If you have found yourself in the heat of a roaring and relentless fire, you can be assured that God, your Silversmith, will never leave you alone in the fire. In the fire, His goal is that He would see His own reflection in your life while He prepares you for a greater work than you could ever imagine.

The Wilderness Before the Fire

The children of Israel had been under bondage for four hundred years as slaves, and they had endured cruel and heartless conditions under Egyptian rule. God was about to do a great work in their midst through a man by the name of Moses. Moses was a man of impatience and anger; he had killed an Egyptian who had been beating one of the Hebrew slaves. Because his impetuous temper had led him to murder, Moses then spent forty years in the wilderness hiding from Pharaoh and tending his father-in-law's sheep.

A wilderness experience has the capacity to devalue a human in his own estimation; a wilderness experience also holds the ability to incite the fictional notion that God is unable to use a person who is a wilderness-dweller. Years of life under arid, barren conditions can rob a man or a woman of valued self-esteem and of the ability to dream. If your wilderness has destroyed your hope and joy, perhaps it is time for you to dream again. Perhaps it is time for you to meet your God in a fire.

So God heard their groaning; and God remembered His covenant with Abraham, Isaac, and Jacob. God saw the sons of Israel, and God took notice of them.—Exodus 2:24–25

If the wilderness has been your spiritual address for far too long, this is an exciting Scripture for you! *God heard . . . God remembered . . . God saw . . . God took notice!* Because we serve a God who never changes, you can be sure that God has heard your particular groaning and prayers . . . God has not forgotten His promises to you . . . God sees what you are going through . . . and God has taken notice of your individual life. When you mistakenly believe and outrageously feel that you are a victim of your circumstances and believe that you have been a wilderness-dweller far too long, always remember that you serve a God who listens . . . He remembers . . . He sees. . . and He is taking note of the things that concern you!

Whenever God is preparing to do a great work through a man or woman at their moment in history, often they must spend some time in the wilderness in order to refine their perception of who God is. An encounter with the Silversmith and with the fire is usually an important stop in the wilderness journey. The Silversmith longs to get your attention, even while in the waste places of life, and His only motive in visiting the fire with you is to rid you of impurities and to see His reflection in your significant life.

The Silversmith who is holding you up for inspection has heard your cries, He remembers His promises to you, He sees what you have been through, and He has taken notice of your precious life! The transformation of time spent in the fire always prepares a vessel of the Lord for a greater work.

COMFORTABLE YET BORING

Now Moses was pasturing the flock of Jethro his father-in-law, the priest of Midian; and he led the flock to the west side of the wilderness and came to Horeb, the mountain of God.—Exodus 3:1

Moses was in his comfortable yet boring rut this day of his wilderness life. There was nothing new to discuss or to think about day after meaningless day. Moses had lived in the wilderness for just under forty years, and his life had taken on the colorless existence of the beige sand and the graying rocks. Moses had lived for 14,600 days with sheep dung between his formerly royal toes, hearing stupid sheep bleat relentlessly in stereo, and having sheep drool on his not-so-princely robes. Moses had never grown accustomed to the endless "baa-baa" of sheep in surround sound that echoed through the desert canyons. Moses had no one with half a brain to converse with, but just day after agonizingly long day of dust, dirt, and rocks.

Moses' feet were perpetually bleeding, his thirst was never quenched, and he never felt quite clean. Living in the wilderness and taking care of sheep that didn't even belong to him was some ending for a boy raised in the palace. Day after day . . . week after week . . . month after month . . . year after year . . . of looking at sheep's behinds.

The angel of the Lord appeared to him in a blazing fire from the midst of a bush; and he looked, and behold, the bush was burning with fire, yet the bush was not consumed.—Exodus 3:2

As Moses looked into the distance, past the smelly wool of the livestock under his care, something bright caught his eye. Moses, this man of the palace and of the wilderness, perceived that a bush was on fire, but that it was not being decimated. There was no charring or pieces falling off the burning bush, but only bright, green leaves in the midst of the vibrant, brilliant fire. The bush was not dry or brittle, nor was it ashy or black, but it was glowing with flames and with the promise of spring.

So Moses said, "I must turn aside now and see this marvelous sight, why the bush is not burned up."—Exodus 3:3

Moses stopped in his incredulous tracks and then turned off the path that he was on in order to investigate this amazing scene in the otherwise ordinary desert. The marvelous sight captured his attention in a way that perhaps nothing had for nearly forty years.

Things do not "just" happen in life, because we do not

live as victims of a random universe where no one is left in charge and the inhabitants thereof are left to fate. There is a God-arranged plan for this world of ours that includes a specific and God-ordained plan for your life even while you hang out in the wilderness. It was not by accident that Moses came upon this burning bush, because God had chosen this particular spot on this particular day to set on fire this particular bush to capture the attention of this particular man. Through every ordinary day and every mundane moment there is a God who is constantly seeking to capture your attention. God wants you out of your rut and out of your wilderness; if it takes a fire to capture your attention, then God will use that fire to speak clearly to you.

ATTENTION!

> *When the Lord saw that he turned aside to look, God called to him from the midst of the bush and said, "Moses, Moses!" And he said, "Here I am."*—Exodus 3:4

It was *when* God saw that He had attracted the attention of the ex-prince Moses that He called him by his name. When God finally sees that He has your attention, He will lovingly but definitively call you by your name.

Craig and I had two lively, rambunctious, darling precocious little boys when I became pregnant with our third child. This third pregnancy ended at twelve weeks, when the baby died inside my womb. My next pregnancy ended at fifteen weeks in utero, and the next pregnancy ended at sixteen weeks in utero, when the babies died inside my womb. Two more successive pregnancies also ended when the babies died inside me at twenty weeks and at sixteen weeks. After losing the third baby, on the way home from the hospital one stormy March night, I looked at my husband, Craig, and said, "God has my attention now. I want to learn what He is trying to show me."

63

Although I never believed that God caused my babies to die, I knew that He could use these tragic early deaths to do a great work in my life. Craig and I both determined in that moment to listen to God with more intentionality than ever before and to yield our hearts completely to Him in the middle of our grief and pain. God used the fire of sending five babies to Heaven with the purpose of doing the greatest work that has ever been done in my life. I would go through the searing pain and the blazing disappointment all over again to be the woman that I am today.

I learned to worship in spite of the fire during those dark, disappointing days of empty arms, dashed hopes, and unending doctor's appointments. I knew that even though my circumstances had changed, my God had not changed. When the fourth baby went to Heaven at twenty weeks in the pregnancy, Craig began to sing over me in the Duke University Hospital delivery room. With tears rolling down his handsome cheeks, as the nurse walked away with our miniature, lifeless child, Craig sang,

"I love You, Lord; and I lift my voice!
To worship You, oh my soul, rejoice!
Take joy, my King, in what You hear;
Let it be a sweet, sweet sound in Your ear."

What does it take to capture your attention? How will God be able to jar you out of your rut? The God who never changes, who is the same yesterday, today, and forever, still uses burning bushes to arrest the attention of His children who have lingered far too long in the wilderness of life. When God is in the fire, there will be no destruction or decimation that takes place; the only purpose for the confrontation of a burning bush is for a man or woman to change direction and listen to the voice of God.

Theologians have a name for a fire of this sort; they often call it a "theophonic" fire. A theophonic fire is a place where God speaks and where His voice is clearly heard. God will use anything and everything, including a burning thornbush, to grab your heart and your attention. God will speak to you from the fire; will you listen to His voice? There are more theophonic moments in life than we can imagine, but often we ignore them and turn away from the fire to escape it. God is speaking . . . He has arrived , . . He is not silent.

The response of Moses should be the response of you and of I when we are confronted by the voice of God from a blazing fire. Moses replied, *"Here I am, Lord."* Rather than question God or argue with God, the vital response of a man or a woman who longs to be used by the Lord will be, *"Here I am, Lord."* If you are disgusted with wilderness living and desire to go from merely surviving to thriving, you will humbly respond, *"Here I am, Lord."* When a fire of questionable origin causes you to turn from your intended pathway, perhaps the best response is, *"Here I am, Lord."*

"Here I am, Lord," is all that God desires to hear from one of His own in the wasteland of life. *"Here I am, Lord,"* is God's desired response whenever a man or a woman faces an unexpected but valuable fire.

HOLY MOMENTS

Then He said, "Do not come near here; remove your sandals from your feet, for the place on which you are standing is holy ground."—Exodus 3:5

Theophonic fires have the potential for becoming the most holy moments of our lives. A fire is meant to be a sacred place where a wilderness dweller is allowed to meet with the God of the universe, the Christ of the Cross, and the Holy Spirit of Pentecost. Never underestimate the probability of meeting the divine presence of God and hearing the powerful voice of God in the fires of your life. The word *"holy"* actually means "a thing consecrated to God." You serve a God so loving and so powerful that He longs to meet with you in the fires that are encountered while living in dry and barren places. God is so powerfully good that He is able to miraculously remove the potential for destruction from the fire that was meant to devastate our lives, and then He meets with us there. God is waiting to talk to you from the fire that has sprung up in the pathway of life. God declares over the searing, roaring flames of your life, "This is a holy moment."

God forbids Satan from using the fire to decimate the life of His child, and then God claims the fire as His very own. God speaks through the roar and intensity of the fire and gathers His child into His arms while lovingly calling his or her name. There are moments in life that were made for consecration to God; a raging fire is one of those moments. Rather than whine and complain and wonder why you must be subjected to the fire, perhaps the best choice you could make is simply to say, *"Here I am, Lord."* God desires that you would recognize His authority in the fire and would understand that it is He who is speaking to you. God is able to use a fire as the place of the greatest turnaround of your life, if you will simply listen and respond, *"Here I am, Lord."*

God told Moses that the ground on which they were meeting was "holy" ground. The word *"holy"*, that is used in Exodus 3:5 to describe the ground upon which Moses walked is the same word that is used in the Bible to describe the innermost part of the Temple, where the Shekinah glory of God appeared. The innermost section of the Temple was where God spoke to the priests who served Him. God speaks to present-day priests through the fires of life, and then God declares that the appointment where He meets with His child is a holy moment. God is able to take every one of our fires and turn them into temples! He can transform any fire that is encountered into the holy inner court of His presence, where He speaks to His beloved child.

> *He said also, "I am the God of your father, the God of Abraham, the God of Isaac, and the God of Jacob." Then Moses hid his face, for he was afraid to look at God.*—Exodus 3:6

God confronted the lonely, angry Moses with His true identity from the depth of the fire. God used this theophonic moment to remind Moses that he was a Hebrew man who shared the lineage of some of the greatest men who had ever lived. In that moment, not only was God reminding Moses of who he was, but He was also alluding to the unspoken fact that He was the God of men who had failed and yet was still able to use the lives of imperfect people in His magnificent plan. Abraham, Isaac, and Jacob were not perfect men, and yet God chose to use them to accomplish extraordinary things for the Kingdom of God. We serve the God of ordinary men who have accomplished supernatural things with their lives. Whenever God speaks to one of His children from the fire, He always confronts the identity of that child and then affirms the truth that He is able to use us in spite of our humanity. The fire, without fail, creates a man or a woman of great usefulness to the plan of God. God takes the fire that was meant to cause destruction, but He uses the fire to only burn away impurities. God is then able to see the reflection of Himself in the life of the believer who has been changed by the fire.

GOD IS ON IT!

> *The Lord said, "I have surely seen the affliction of My people who are in Egypt, and have given heed to their*

*cry because of their taskmasters, for I am aware of their
suerings. So I have come down to deliver them from
the power of the Egyptians, and to bring them up from
that land to a good and spacious land, to a land flowing
with milk and honey, to the place of the Canaanite
and the Hittite and the Amorite and the Perizzite and
the Hivite and the Jebusite."*—Exodus 3:7–8

And in these two Old Testament verses, God shares His
heart with the lives of every wilderness dweller who will ever
live in all of history! God has surely seen what you are facing
today and has heard your individual cry. God is aware of your
personal suffering and is on His way to deliver you from the
power of the enemy! God promises to bring you up to a land
of promise and blessing! You will not be a wilderness-dweller
for long, because God is on it! He has not forgotten you, nor
has He ignored the cry of your heart.

If you have ever doubted the heart of God toward His
children, linger on these words one more time: *"I have surely
seen . . . I have given heed . . . I am aware . . . I have come
down to deliver . . . and to bring them up!"* What a promise!
What a God!

It is in the fire when God has captured the attention of
His wilderness-dwelling child, that He is able at last to share
His plan in full.

WHO AM I?

*"Now, behold, the cry of the sons of Israel has come
to Me; furthermore, I have seen the oppression with
which the Egyptians are oppressing them. Therefore,
come now, and I will send you to Pharaoh, so that you
may bring My people, the sons of Israel, out of Egypt."
But Moses said to God, "Who am I, that I should go*

to Pharaoh, and that I should bring the sons of Israel out of Egypt?"—Exodus 3:9–11

God had already promised Moses that **He Himself** would certainly deliver the children of Israel out of Egypt, and all that Moses was required to do was to go to Pharaoh and inform the king of Egypt of God's superior plan. However, Moses began to wilt into his wilderness-induced insecurity, and then he started to argue with God.

"Who am I?" was the fearful question of Moses. Moses had instantly forgotten that God Himself was going to deliver the Hebrew nation and that Moses was merely an instrument in the purposes and plans of God. The wilderness had pulverized this man into a midget in his faith, and all he could think about was his own insignificance. Moses was ignoring the miraculous fact that God had promised that His presence and His power would always be with Moses the man!

However, before we shred Moses with our criticism, let's take just a moment for self-examination. Have you ever questioned God's choice of in you? Have you ever wondered whether or not God knows what He is doing on any given day of your life? The picture of Moses standing in the wilderness in front of a burning bush is also, unfortunately, a vivid picture of you and of me. We are the immature children who are foolish enough to argue with God, the Creator of the universe.

The next time you choose to argue with God, remember Who is going to win! The next time you choose to remind God of how worthless you are, listen to Him remind you of how worthy He is! The next time you dare to give God a human-conceived suggestion, remind yourself that Father knows best! How does a human falsely believe that it is possible to bring one morsel of information to the throne room that He has not already considered? How foolish of all of us! The created one should never be audacious and selfish enough to argue with the Creator!

This man, Moses, had received an exemplary Egyptian education and had been raised to be the next king of Egypt. Elocution had likely been part of his prestigious academic rigors. Moses had been taught by the experts of the day how to speak clearly and how to persuade passionately so that people would recognize his authority and leadership skills. Knowing that Moses was well-prepared for leadership and for public speaking, why did this man argue with God? It is incredible that Moses would look at his life and sadly lament, *"I can't . . . I'm not enough . . . I'll never be . . ."*

The only possible cause of the insecurity that Moses had embraced was the effect of the time that he had spent in the wilderness. The wilderness has a habit of chipping away at one's self-esteem and then fertilizing the doubts in one's life. The wilderness experience in the life of Moses, for forty years, had shouted into Moses' heart, *"You are not . . . you can't . . . you will never be . . ."*

The power of God lies in the evidence that He is able to use the flames of a fire to counteract the curse of the wilderness. Into your wilderness today God shouts His presence, His power, His availability, and His call upon your life.

Moses was educated in all the learning of the Egyptians and he was a man of power in words and deeds.—Acts 7:22

The Holy Spirit had the correct view of what Moses was capable of accomplishing for the purposes and plans of God. God had used the entire life of Moses as preparation for this one unforgettable moment in time. The Holy Spirit also has a correct view of what you, my friend, are capable of accomplishing for the Kingdom of God. Your entire life has been in preparation for the calling and the destiny of God on your life. It is a divine necessity for you not to believe what the wilderness says about you, but to wholeheartedly come into agreement with what God says about you.

Until Moses encountered Him at the burning bush, God had only been a God of history to him and not a God of the present tense. Moses had absolute certainty that God had miraculously worked in the lives of Abraham, Isaac, and Jacob. Moses never would have questioned the validity of the biographical and historical accounts of this triumvirate of champions of the faith. Yet at this significant moment in the life of Moses, when God had actually chosen to defy nature and speak through a burning bush that was not being decimated, Moses blew it! All of history had worked itself to this climactic moment—when Moses whined, *"I can't . . . I'm not enough . . . I'll never be . . ."*

Moses failed to understand the sacredness of this moment, and he turned it into a selfish moment. The fire that is experienced in the wilderness of life will either be viewed as sacred or be clutched on to as selfish, but it will not be both.

Unfortunately, the similarities between Moses and you and I have not been thoroughly exhausted yet. Like Moses, we have no problem believing that the Bible is historically accurate in every way through every word. We believe that God opened the Red Sea, that He spared Daniel in the lions' den, and that Jesus fed five thousand men and their families with only five hard rolls and two sardines. We believe that as certainly as George Washington was America's first president, Peter walked on water, Lazarus was raised from the dead, and that those three Hebrew boys didn't even smell like smoke. However, when confronted with the possibility of God working in *us* and through *us*, we respond like Moses did: *"I can't . . . I'm not enough . . . I'll never be . . ."*

When God proclaims through a burning bush that He is well able to restore a miserable marriage, create a new job, or heal a broken and diseased body, often we respond, *"Are You sure You can use me? But I am so ordinary!"* One of the miraculous determinants of a burning bush is that it settles the argument of whether your God is merely a God of history or a God of the present tense.

WHO ARE YOU?!

And He said, "Certainly I will be with you, and this shall be the sign to you that it is I who have sent you: when you have brought the people out of Egypt, you shall worship God at this mountain." Then Moses said to God, "Behold, I am going to the sons of Israel, and I will say to them, 'The God of your fathers has sent me to you.' Now they may say to me, 'What is His name?' What shall I say to them?"—Exodus 3:12–13

Finally! The first intelligent words that the insecure, incredulous Moses has uttered: *"Who are You, God?"* And with this eternal question, the true purpose of the fire in the wilderness is revealed. A burning bush experience becomes glorious when a believer becomes acquainted with who God is! God reveals His identity, His character, and His name to men and women who are willing to stand in front of a burning bush. The same God who saved the life of Moses as an infant and the same God who allowed Moses to be raised in the palace was about to introduce Himself and His plans to a wilderness dweller by the name of Moses.

God said to Moses, "I AM WHO I AM"; and He said, "Thus you shall say to the sons of Israel, 'I AM has sent me to you.'" God, furthermore, said to Moses, "Thus you shall say to the sons of Israel, 'The Lord, the God of your fathers, the God of Abraham, the God of Isaac, and the God of Jacob, has sent me to you.' This is My name forever, and this is My memorial-name to all generations."—Exodus 3:14–15

God identified Himself to Moses in a powerful and distinctly new manner in these verses. No longer did Moses need to wonder who the God of the burning bush was or to whom he was talking. There would be no mistake from that point forward in Moses' life who was instructing him, leading him, and empowering him. "I Am" was the greatest voice that Moses had ever heard. No longer would Moses be identified by the palace or by the wilderness, but from that moment forward, Moses would be identified by the God who is known as "I AM."

It is interesting to note the precise Hebrew words that God chose to identify Himself with and the tense in which they were used. God specifically chose the phrase, *"I Am Who I Am,"* which is from the imperfect stem of the Hebrew verb "to be." The imperfect tense denotes an action started in the past, continuing in the present, and not yet complete in the future. God was declaring to the man Moses, "I am who I have always been and will continue to be!" The "to be" verb in any language literally means "to exist or to have life." God was instructing Moses that God has always existed, that He was alive and well in the current wilderness of Moses' life, and that He would continue to exist and be an active part of Moses' life in the future!

God was clearly not a figment of the overactive imagination of Moses, nor was God the main character in Moses' desert-induced hallucinations. God was reminding Moses that He did not exist because people desperately hoped that God was real and wished mightily for His existence. There is no "might" or "perhaps" concerning the existence of our God. He was . . . He is . . . and He will always be!

Whatever you are going through or facing today, remind yourself that *God has seen . . . He is seeing . . . and He will continue to see! God has heard . . . He is hearing . . . and He will continue to hear! God has been aware . . . He is aware . . . and He will continue to be aware! God has delivered . . . God is delivering . . . and God will continue to deliver!*

The Bible alone promises the singular solutions to all of our problems, to all of our wilderness experiences, to all of our confrontations with the fires of life, and to all of our *"Why God?! Why do I have to go through this?"* moments in life. The Bible, through the voice of God to Moses, presents Jehovah as the God of the present tense who is continually being God to His children. God is the present-tense answer to everything you ever have needed, everything you need today, and everything you ever will need in life. Whatever you need today, He is "I Am"!

There are some Hebrew scholars who translate this name of God as *"I am the Is-ing One!"* What joy there is in knowing that we serve a God who always is! In times of sickness, He is our Healer; in times of lack, He is our Provider. When life is confusing and chaotic, He is our Peace; and when depression and gloom set in, He is our Joy!

You have all of God at your daily disposal and as your constant Companion and Friend. The name "Jehovah," which is introduced here for the very first time in Scripture, is always used with the revelation of God. When the Old Testament references that God is speaking, as in the phrase, *"Thus says Jehovah . . . ,"* it is always the name "Jehovah" that is used. God not only exists in the past, present, and future tense, but He speaks in the past, present, and future tense, as well. We serve a God who is still speaking and revealing Himself to His children today!

HE HAS BEEN TO YOUR FUTURE!

"Go and gather the elders of Israel together and say to them, 'The Lord, the God of your fathers, the God of Abraham, Isaac and Jacob, has appeared to me, saying, "I am indeed concerned about you and what has been done to you in Egypt. So I said, I will bring you up out of the affliction of Egypt to the land of the Canaanite and the Hittite and the Amorite and the Perizzite and the Hivite and the Jebusite, to a land flowing with milk and honey."' They will pay heed to what you say; and you with the elders of Israel will come to the king of Egypt and you will say to him, 'The Lord, the God of the Hebrews, has met with us. So now, please, let us go a three days' journey into the wilderness, that we may sacrifice to the Lord our God.' But I know that the king of Egypt will not permit you to go, except under compulsion. So I will stretch out My hand and strike Egypt with all My miracles which I shall do in the midst of it; and after that he will let you go."—Exodus 3:16–20

God audibly prophesied the future of Moses, the future of the children of Israel, and the future of Egypt to Moses in these significant and familiar verses. As believers who are knowledgeable of this Sunday school story, we are tempted to read these verses with a bit of disinterest, because we know all that Moses has to go through. We all know about the plagues, the parting of the Red Sea, and being lost in the wilderness. But may I just remind you that Moses had not watched *The Ten Commandments* with Charlton Heston, and he had not taken his boys to see the cinematic version of *The Prince of*

Egypt! Moses did not know what his future held, just like you, my friend, are not aware of what your future holds. But you serve the God of Moses who has been to your future—and it is good! God sees in advance, and He is able to make a way where there seems to be no way. We know that the God of Moses is a good God and that He exists to constantly work good in all of our life situations. Therefore, He has indeed been to the future and has enthusiastically stamped your future with the word, *Good!*

The story of this fugitive, Moses, who was on the run and who then hid in the wilderness, serves as an exciting reminder that whenever one encounters a fire, "I Am" will be there, because He never takes His caring eyes off His children for one instant of time. If you are running away from life and from the consequences of sin, God is there. If you have found yourself in the wilderness with no direction, God is there. We know that if we listen, we will hear His loving voice speaking above the roar of the fire. We also know that the fires encountered by a child of God this side of Heaven have no power of destruction or decimation. A fire is the wonderful place where God reveals Himself to weary wilderness dwellers and where He speaks purpose and destiny. A fire was fashioned by God to be the most sacred moment in the life of a believer.

CHAPTER 10
IS IT GOLD YET?

DID YOU KNOW that there is more than one type of gold present in the world? The exact type and value of gold is unable to be determined until it has been exposed to fire. Fire has the ability to reveal the quality of gold that is in one's possession.

White and rose gold are generally mixed with other, less expensive metals. These two types of gold both look beautiful and can actually be used for many things, but when placed in the fire, what is then visible in the white and rose gold are the impurities and the inexpensive alloys that have risen to the top due to the heat of the fire.

There is also the proverbial "fool's gold," which is merely a yellow metal and has no chemical substance of pure gold in its makeup. "Fool's gold" may look like the real deal, but when carefully examined, it contains no inherent qualities of pure gold. However, there is no way to ascertain whether it is pure gold or "fool's gold" until it is placed in the fire. Blazing heat is the only way that a jeweler, silversmith, or goldsmith is able to identify the type of gold in his or her possession.

Pure gold is always yellow and contains no alloys or other substances in its makeup. Pure gold can only come from pure gold. It is impossible to manufacture pure gold from any other substance than the pure gold itself. And, most magnificently of all, when pure gold is placed in the fire, all you are able to see is the reflection of the Refiner! All you see is Him! Becoming a pure gold Christian entails reflecting only the glory of God in our lives. Becoming a pure gold Christian means that I must certainly decrease and that He and His glory must increase in my life daily.

THE REFINER'S FIRE

Unfortunately, there are times when the Refiner's fire is of no avail, and when we, His children, resist the refining process of God. There are times in life, because of our resistance, when the fire reveals our ugliness rather than our beauty. Instead of allowing the fire to do its refining work in our lives, we hang on to anger, selfishness, pride, and opinions, and we refuse to let those impurities be released from our lives.

The bellows blow fiercely, the lead is consumed by the fire; in vain the refining goes on, but the wicked are not separated. They call them rejected silver, because the Lord has rejected them.—Jeremiah 6:29–30

The prophet Jeremiah recounts the troubling biography of one who resists the Refiner's fire. The fire burns on and on, but the dross and imperfections are never released and removed. The Smith is never able to see His reflection in the piece of metal that has resisted its potential to become anything of value. Instead, this particular piece of metal has stubbornly hung on to and clung to that which cheapens it, regardless of the intensity of the heat. This stubborn piece of silver, referenced by the prophet Jeremiah, by necessity is rejected for use by the refiner because it is impure, unusable, and unattractive. God, as the Master Refiner, allows a piece of silver or gold to be placed in the fire time after time, and when the dross is stubbornly held on to, the refining process continues in vain.

This story, found in Jeremiah, has a tragic ending. This obstinate and impure piece of silver has been set aside because it insisted on hanging on to its weaknesses. Oh, how I don't want to be set aside by God! I want God to be able to use me every day in every possible way! I want less of me and less impurities in my life! I want more of Him to replace all that was me and all of my weaknesses, both visible and invisible. There is no more tragic and horrifying phrase than for a Christian to hear from the Father's heart, *I simply am unable to use you. You have refused to let go of that which weakens you.*

The Refiner's fire is able to miraculously transform worthless junk into a commodity that possesses the value of pure gold to God who first created the precious substance. The recycling process of God always takes place under relentless pressure and is accompanied by searing heat while the fire is tended by the Refiner Himself. He takes the natural issues of our lives, touches them with His "super," and we miraculously become "supernatural." A miracle takes place while in the fire: We become like Him! We reflect His brilliant glory! He sees Himself in you and in me! And then, He is able to use us to build His sanctuary.

> *"And I heard a loud voice from the throne saying, 'Now the dwelling of God is with men, and He will live with them. They will be His people, and God Himself will be with them and be their God.'"*—Revelation 21:3

GOD'S ADDRESS

Your life was created to be God's own dwelling place. He no longer frustratingly appears sporadically in a temple made of bricks and mortar as He did during the days of the Old Testament, but He lives eternally in the hearts and lives of His children. God is deeply concerned about the place where He lives, and the materials with which He builds His temple are of utmost importance to Him.

> *Do you not know that you are a temple of God and that the Spirit of God dwells in you?*—1 Corinthians 3:16

Your life is the earthly address where God lives, and He is

genuinely concerned about the condition of His home. Your life should be a home fit for the grandest of all kings, because that is who He is and your life is where He has chosen to live. Rest assured that God is not on a search for a prestigious and impressive address, nor is He on the hunt for the trappings of creature comforts. However, God is passionately and thoroughly inspecting our human lives in order to discover purity and cleanliness. God is not looking for human talents, expensive furnishings, or exquisite accoutrements, but He is diligently scouting for hearts of pure gold.

> *But the Lord said to Samuel, "Do not look at his appearance or at the height of his stature, because I have rejected him; for God sees not as man sees, for man looks at the outward appearance, but the Lord looks at the heart."*—1 Samuel 16:7

If you mistakenly believe that your gifts, talents, or abilities are the most valuable prerequisites that enable you to live a life of pure gold, perhaps you should think again. If you hope that your achievements, awards, or bank accounts give your life pure-gold status, perhaps you should consider again. If you falsely imagine that your weight, marital status, or academic degrees determine the extent of your pure-gold validity, my friend, ponder again!

For a man or a woman to live a life of pure gold, it entails an inner work that only the Father is able to accomplish. Knowing that your life is the actual dwelling place of God, you must allow Him to do His deep remodeling in your life.

The sanctuary that is described in the Old Testament is a prophetic look at the components and priorities that are valued in the New Testament sanctuary or temple. The Old Testament sanctuary is meant to be a foreshadowing of all that you are able to become in Him. What a grand possibility! It is vital to study the Old Testament tabernacle and then to apply the principles found in that study to the lives that you and I are living today. It has always been among the chief concerns of God the Father that His children build and therefore provide a suitable house for His glorious presence.

GOD'S HOUSE

"Let them construct a sanctuary for Me, that I may dwell among them."—Exodus 25:8

God spoke these specific words of divine instruction to the children of Israel who were confined to the wilderness by the consequence of their own choices. They had not yet arrived at the Promised Land, which was also known as Canaan. It was in the middle of the wilderness of their own choosing that God instructed them to build a sanctuary fit for a King. What a strange place to build a tabernacle . . . in the middle of nowhere! Would God, the Creator of the universe, the Chief Engineer of the redwood forest, the Designer of the lush tropics of Hawaii, and the Architect of the magnificent fjords, actually require that His children build a home for Him in a desert?! A desert is an arid and dry place with no beautiful vegetation, no lush greenery, and no brilliant flora, and yet God chose a wilderness for His habitation.

Surely the God of Niagara Falls, the French Riviera, and the Amazon River could have chosen a more desirable location for His permanent dwelling place upon Earth! Why didn't God choose a busy city with a massive amount of traffic that would be more accessible to a greater population group? Once again, as humanity we find ourselves questioning God and His motives. Rather than ask the impertinent question of, *"Why here?"* perhaps a more meaningful question would be this: *"God, why do You desire to build a sanctuary?"*

God desired to construct a sanctuary so that He would have a place to dwell among His dearly loved children. The place where God chooses to meet with and talk to His children becomes the sacred place of His presence. The literal definition of the word *tabernacle* is *"the designated place where God meets with His people."* The reason God is intentionally concerned with the building of His tabernacle is because it is where His glory dwells. In addition to the receptacle of His Shekinah glory, the tabernacle was always meant to be the primary place where mankind would have the opportunity to fellowship with the glory of God. The tabernacle of God is the place where God's children offer up the sacrifices of expensive and well-chosen offerings, and it is also the place where they worship Him with great celebration and with wholehearted participation. The Temple has always been, and will always be, of primary importance to Father God, because His one priority is to develop relationship with those who call Him *"Dad."*

The most important business and work of every generation takes place not in boardrooms or on Wall Street; the legacy and greatest heritage of a generation takes place not in the halls of academia or in the United Nations; the most important and lasting work of every generation takes place in the tabernacle. The tabernacle is, quite simply, the place where God enjoys the company of His children!

God has definite and eternal opinions concerning the appearance of His tabernacle, the materials with which it is constructed, and the activities that take place there.

"Make this tabernacle and all its furnishings exactly like the pattern I will show you."—Exodus 25:9 NIV

God required a strict building code and exact attention to the details of His instructions concerning the building of the

Old Testament tabernacle. The tabernacle then was not to stray from God's specific and holy blueprint, nor is the tabernacle now allowed to stray from God's plan. The detailed instructions that God provided were never meant to be burdensome or legalistic, but to demonstrate the God-given truth that people can only come to God on His terms, not on human terms.

What does your life look like? Are you ready for God to build something new in you? Your life is the dwelling place of God the Father, Jesus, His dear Son, and the powerful Holy Spirit! Perhaps it is time for you and me to consider the possibility of allowing God, the greatest Architect ever, to remodel the content of our lives.

CHAPTER 11
RED + BLACK = GOLD

TWO SPECIFIC ITEMS in the Old Testament tabernacle of Moses were required to be made of the purest of gold. These two items were the mercy seat and the lampstand. There were other items in the tabernacle that were overlaid with pure gold, but none that were required to be solely made of pure gold all the way through to the inner core as were the lampstand and the mercy seat.

As a point of review, remember that the Old Testament tabernacle is a prophetic look at the requirements of the New Testament dwelling place of God, which is *you*! As we study the mercy seat and the lampstand of the Old Testament tabernacle, their importance and usefulness in the life that you are presenting to God will be ultimately visible.

"You shall make a mercy seat of pure gold, two and a half cubits long and one and a half cubits wide."—Exodus 25:17

THE GRACE PLACE

The mercy seat was located in the Ark of the Covenant, which was the most holy place in the entire tabernacle. The beloved term *mercy seat* means "the seat of grace," or "the location of grace." When defined by itself, the word *mercy* specifically means "thing of wiping out, thing of cleaning, to cover over." The mercy seat was the place where the sin of the people was wiped out and where the blood of the sacrifice covered the sin. The mercy seat, located in the Holy of Holies, was the place where the blood of a lamb was sprinkled in the presence of Yahweh.

Two cherubim, upon whose outstretched wings God dwelled in a cloud, were placed on both ends of the mercy seat. The beautiful and glorious mercy seat was where the highest and most perfect act of atonement took place for all mankind. As already noted, the mercy seat was one of two pieces of furniture in the tabernacle that God required to be made of pure gold.

If you long to live a pure-gold life, and if your heart's desire is to offer God a vibrant and strong dwelling place, you must encounter the mercy seat of God. Pure gold is only extracted from pure gold; your life will never be a pure-gold dwelling place until you extract the pure-gold attributes from the place of mercy. This is a place where sins are forgiven and where the blood of a Lamb covers all of your human shortcomings. As New Covenant believers, pure gold is only extracted from the blood of Calvary. The sprinkling of the blood of the Lamb is what miraculously turns your life into a pure-gold existence. It may not make physical or chemical sense, but the theological truth is found in this equation:

RED (BLOOD OF JESUS) + BLACK (YOUR SINS) = PURE GOLD

It is impossible for a man or woman to offer to God a pure-gold life merely by being religious, by doing good works, or by putting on a good front. All of those offerings are mere fool's gold, and God is definitely smart enough to discern the difference! There is an endless list of pieces of fool's gold that mankind has tried to offer to God in place of pure gold; perhaps you have tried it some of them yourself. Have you tried to impress God with wealth, education, travel, social work, or piety? God knows fool's gold when He sees it, and He will not tolerate anything less than pure gold in His dwelling place. You are His dwelling place, and it is vital that you throw away the fool's gold and replace it with pure gold. The only place where you can attain pure gold is by encountering the mercy seat of the Lamb. It is inadvisable to try to come to God on your own terms; He is the One who drew the blueprint for the construction of your temple. You must build your life with attention to and compliance with His engineering.

The glory of the birthplace of pure gold is discovered when a man or woman who encounters the mercy seat of the Lamb, then becomes a seat of mercy for the cause of Jesus Christ! Your life was created to be a place of mercy, where the sins of others are covered by the blood of Jesus Christ. As Christ has forgiven you, you are now able to forgive others! Your life, in the deepest and most holy part, is a place where love covers and forgives. People are safe and forgiven in the place of grace that is offered by your life because you have determined to be a pure-gold furnishing in the Temple of God.

Above all, keep fervent in your love for one another, because love covers a multitude of sins.—1 Peter 4:8

LET IT GO!

One afternoon, the disciples asked Jesus to teach them how to pray. This, of course, must have been music to the ears of the One who had spent eternity past in heaven listening to the prayers of humanity. Jesus had learned a thing or two about effective prayer while hanging out in the throne room with God the Father, and from that wonderful, powerful Holy Spirit who teaches us all how to pray!

As the disciples listened, Jesus perhaps had a faraway look in His eyes as He pondered what it had been like to be on the receiving end of prayer. And on this day, Jesus taught these men how to pray words that would be heard in the throne of heaven and would capture the Father's attention and response.

> *"Our Father who is in heaven,*
> *Hallowed be Your name.*
> *Your kingdom come.*
> *Your will be done,*
> *On earth as it is in heaven.*
> *Give us this day our daily bread.*
> *And forgive us our debts, as we also have forgiven*
> *our debtors.*
> *And do not lead us into temptation, but deliver us*
> *from evil. [For Yours is the kingdom and the power*
> *and the glory forever. Amen.]"*—Matthew 6:9–13

Jesus then paused and looked around at the rapt faces of the men who sat at His feet, and He knew in that moment that He needed to reiterate a prayer point while He had their full and heartfelt attention.

> *"For if you forgive others for their transgressions, your*
> *heavenly Father will also forgive you. But if you do*
> *not forgive others, then your Father will not forgive*
> *your transgressions."*—Matthew 6:14–15

Forgiveness was the singular point that Jesus chose to emphasize outside of the context of the prayer that He taught to His band of brothers. The word that Jesus carefully chose to communicate the power of forgiveness was the Greek word *aphiemi.* This word means "to set free; to let go, to release; to liberate completely."

You and I do not have the privilege of holding others hostage to their past actions and words. We are obligated, as a mercy seat made of pure gold, to let it go! As the mercy seat in the temple of God, it is imperative that you rid yourself of the spirit of offense and no longer hold onto other people's shortcomings or sins. As the mercy seat, you must give up your right to think about how others have wronged you, as well as talking about how they have mistreated you or hurt you. Let it go! If you are still thinking about or talking about an old offense done to you, it is because you have not totally forgiven the person who wronged you. You are not responding like the pure-gold mercy seat that you have been called to be. Let it go!

If you refuse to forgive and then you choose to continue to discuss, debate, and rehash other people's shortcomings and failures, your life is in agreement with the devil rather than with the Lord. The devil loves to cause you to forget who you are as the pure-gold mercy seat and engage you in conversations about past hurts and old pain. Let it go!

The father of all lies manipulates and plots to place a mercy seat in situations where you are continually reminded of others' failures. Let it go!

When the enemy realizes that he is unable to engage you in conversation, he will tuck his broken old tail between his scrawny little legs and leave you alone. But as long as you are still biting . . . he is still offering the bait of offense.

If you have truly and completely forgiven a person and are committed to be the personification of the pure-gold mercy seat, you will refuse to drag up past pain and hurt caused by a person from your past. You no longer have the right or privilege to pull out an offense at a later date and use it strategically against someone . . . let it go!

Forgiveness wipes out the transgression, and then love earnestly covers it. The magnificent beauty of forgiveness and the miraculous power of love is that because grace has happened to you, now you have been given the delight of offering it to others. You are now the grace place made of pure gold.

Forgiveness is of utmost importance to God the Father—

it is a pure-gold issue. God sent His Son, Jesus, to die so that those who had been trapped by the ravages of sin could fully experience the forgiveness of the Father. As believers, we must commit to doing things God's way in order to receive the blessings of God. We must build our lives according to the Blueprint of God and not according to the blueprint of self. When I approach the throne of God in prayer with unforgiveness in my heart toward a person who has been made in the image of God, there is a blockage that restricts sweet fellowship with the Father. As God observes the unforgiveness in my heart, He gently and lovingly reminds me, "Forgive the one who has wronged you. Forgive completely. Be who you were created to be . . . the pure-gold mercy seat in the temple of God. When you have forgiven, come back to Me and we will talk about your desires and needs."

If you are a parent, you easily understand this principle of forgiveness. If a child came to you who was angry with his or her sibling and said to you, "I love you so much. Even though I hate my brother, can I still have a brand-new bike?"

Of course you would respond with these wise words, "No, my child. Settle the issue with your brother and restore your relationship with him. When you do, then we will talk about your desires and needs. Forgiveness and relationships are so much more important than temporary desires."

Jesus cares more about our relationships than He is concerned about our material requests. Forgiveness is high on God's list of priorities for your life. As a mercy seat that is made from pure gold, your number-one job description is to demonstrate the characteristics of that golden place of grace.

TO INFINITY AND BEYOND

Then Peter came and said to Him, "Lord, how often shall my brother sin against me and I forgive him?

Up to seven times?" Jesus said to him, "I do not say to you, up to seven times, but up to seventy times seven."—Matthew 18:21–22

The speak-before-you-think Peter was in the habit of impressing people with his great ideas and know-it-all opinions. When he came to Jesus this day, he thought that he had come up with a perfect solution to this challenge of forgiving others. It was a well-established fact that "seven" was the perfect number, and therefore Peter knew that forgiving someone seven times would show a perfect heart. But Jesus wasn't impressed. He is rarely impressed with our human suggestions or opinions. Jesus challenged Peter and said, "Nope. Not seven times. How about seventy times seven, Peter? Can you do that?"

Jesus was not suggesting that it was in Peter's best interest to forgive someone 490 heartfelt times. The phrase "seventy times seven" did not equal 490, but it literally meant "times without number." Jesus told Peter the Pompous that no matter how many times you have forgiven someone, you should do it one more time. Peter was being challenged, by the Lord of the universe, to forgive times without number. There is no ordinal number that would satisfy the quotient that Christ requires. Christ is speaking to your heart today with words of blessing and encouragement: "It is time for you to forgive to *infinity and beyond!"*

When a man or woman encounters the mercy seat of Christ, he or she then becomes the mercy seat. No matter how difficult, cruel, or abusive people have acted toward you, Christ calls you to act like Him and become a person of pure-gold value. I believe that the Lord actually allows difficult people into our lives for a reason: It is part of the defining and refining fire that allows an individual to become pure gold. Christ will never leave you in the pure-gold process, nor will He expect you to do anything that He Himself has not already done. Jesus will carefully watch you as the impurities are burned out of your life, while you are in the fire that has been ignited by difficult people. His goal is to see Himself in you. Your goal is to respond like He would respond. What a beautiful and powerful process this fire has initiated!

> *"But I say to you, love your enemies and pray for those who persecute you, so that you may be sons of your Father who is in heaven; for He causes His sun to rise on the evil and the good, and sends rain on the righteous and the unrighteous."*—Matthew 5:44–45

When you choose to forgive a demanding and contentious person, you are acting just like your Dad, and you will be recognized as a son or daughter of the greatest Forgiver of all eternity! He will be seen in you! You have become like Him! Your life is now defined by the lovely promise that you have become a grace place of pure-gold value.

Why is it that we seem to place great value on stating opinions, demanding our own way, and trampling over other people's feelings? The value system of Earth and the value system of Heaven are mutually exclusive. Heaven's repository is a place where pure-gold decisions are made based upon grace. Will you value what Heaven values? Or will you stubbornly hold on to the cheap fool's gold of Earth? It's up to you.

AN APPOINTMENT WITH GOD

> *"There I will meet with you; and from above the mercy seat, from between the two cherubim which are upon the ark of the testimony, I will speak to you about all that I will give you in commandment for the sons of Israel."*—Exodus 25:22

When a believer encounters the mercy seat, it becomes a

place of divine appointment. It is at the mercy seat that you will hear God's voice and experience His divine presence. God meets with His children at the mercy seat. It is His favorite spot to be with those whom He loves the very most. When you extend the forgiveness of the mercy seat to others, God will meet you there intimately and you will hear His voice. It is at the mercy seat of forgiveness that a son or a daughter of the King becomes the pure-gold representation of Heaven's grandeur.

An appointment with God changes everything about you and for you. An appointment with God changes your capacity to hear His voice and to lavish in His presence. An appointment with God reveals your true destiny and the purpose for which you were made. Go to that grace place and experience His mercy . . . then . . . you must be the place of grace for a world of compromise and sin.

You were not made to be the habitation of cheap impurities or earthly opinion; you were made to be like God in all of your dealings and with all of your heart. What a glorious call and a rich challenge!

CHAPTER 12
THIS LITTLE LIGHT OF MINE

"Then you shall make a lampstand of pure gold."—Exodus 25:31

The mercy seat was not the only item made of pure gold that was found in the tabernacle of the Old Testament. The second item in the tabernacle of God that was made of pure gold was the lampstand, which was the only source of light due to the fact that there were no windows in the tabernacle. This lampstand, known as the *menorah*, was intricately beautiful and extraordinarily detailed in design.

"You shall charge the sons of Israel, that they bring you clear oil of beaten olives for the light, to make a lamp burn continually."—Exodus 27:20

A priest in the house of the Lord attended to the wick of the lampstand and replenished the oil twice every day. He would carefully perform this sacred and holy duty in the morning and again in the evening. The light of the lampstand was never to go out, as a constant reminder that God was with His people continually.

AFRAID OF THE DARK

The Lord is my light and my salvation; whom shall I fear?—Psalm 27:1

Generally the things that we are afraid of, we are afraid of in the dark. When the light chases out the dark, the fear readily disappears, as well. The Lord has continually given His light for every situation on Earth; therefore there is absolutely no reason to be afraid and there is absolutely nothing to fear. Dealing with fear is an issue of pure-gold importance and value.

In order to become the pure-gold lampstand in the house of the Lord, you must allow the Lord to help you overcome your fear and be in perpetual remembrance that the Lord is your light. If fear has paralyzed your life and stolen your ability to move ahead with your plans and dreams, remember that it is the Lord who lights your way, one golden step at a time.

But the path of the righteous is like the light of dawn, that shines brighter and brighter until the full day.—Proverbs 4:18

Just as the mercy seat was a foreshadowing of the work and Person of Jesus Christ, the same prophetic personification is evident in the pure-gold lampstand.

"While I am in the world, I am the Light of the world."—John 9:5

The presence of Jesus Christ assured the world, which was darkened by sin and failure, that never again would people walk in darkness. Jesus shines brighter than the sun, the moon, and the stars, and He is well able to rid your life of darkness and of fear. He came so that darkness would no longer cause you to fall or walk in fear.

The people who walk in darkness will see a great light; those who live in a dark land, the light will shine on them.—Isaiah 9:2

Light changes everything for a people who have only known bleak, black darkness. No longer are we a people who are horrified by what might be lurking around the next corner or petrified by the inky black of living a life of sin, but we have experienced the God who declared over the universe, "Let there be light!"

"I will lead the blind by a way they do not know, in

paths they do not know I will guide them. I will make darkness into light before them and rugged places into plains. These are the things I will do, and I will not leave them undone."—Isaiah 42:16

His divine presence, which always includes light, changes everything for you! Darkness is incapable of cloaking decisions, purpose, or destiny. God has promised to shine His light on every dark area that attempts to swallow your life; He has promised not to leave this promise of light and destiny undone in your life.

YOU ARE THE LIGHT!

Then Jesus again spoke to them, saying, "I am the Light of the world; he who follows Me will not walk in the darkness, but will have the Light of life."—John 8:12

If you have determined to be a follower of Jesus Christ, then you have become the lampstand of the New Testament temple! You are the light that will lead others out of darkness, and His brilliant and eternal light is shining to the world through your life. The world that experiences your presence is no longer a world of black shame or dark fear, but it is a world that is gloriously lit by His light that shines through you. When Jesus left Planet Earth to return to Heaven's streets of pure gold, He left you here to be a pure-gold lampstand.

"You are the light of the world. A city set on a hill cannot be hidden; nor does anyone light a lamp and put it under a basket, but on the lampstand, and it gives light to all who are in the house. Let your light shine before men in such a way that they may see your good works, and glorify your Father who is in heaven."—Matthew 5:14–16

When Jesus returned to the Father's glory, He left behind on Planet Earth an integral part of who He is. He left the joy of His Father's presence on Earth . . . He left the healing power that He had been given on Earth . . . He left the peace that passes understanding on Earth . . . He left the Person and the power of the Holy Spirit on Earth . . . and He left His light and His glory with us, His dearly loved children. Heaven was already bright enough; therefore He generously left with us His power that lights up situations that are dark and foreboding.

It is the oil of the Holy Spirit that enables us to burn with a light brighter than ourselves. It is the oil of the Holy Spirit that gives us the power to light the way for others, to give to others, to share with others what we ourselves have been given, to pray for others, and to be kind to others.

SHINY OR GRUMPY?

The question remains, "Are you shining or not?" Are you grumpy and impatient with those whose lives intersect with your life, or are the majority of your words spoken with patience and love? If there is one thing that is true about light, it is that it attracts bugs! There are thousands of "bugs" out there who need your light and will come running toward you when you simply turn your light up a notch. There are fearful people who have only known darkness in their lives who need your light to show them the way.

Light is a visible substance, and your faith should be visible, as well! It is a pure-gold issue of maximum priority that your light is burning at full strength and is properly cared for. Do you share your faith freely and often? Or have you hidden your faith and your testimony under a bushel of embarrassment? You must shine! You simply must!

RED + BLACK = GOLD

We are now the priests who have been assigned the immense responsibility of ensuring that the light in the tabernacle, which is us, burns day and night without ceasing or without sputtering.

> *Encourage one another day after day, as long as it is still called "Today."*—Hebrews 3:13

The lampstand in the New Testament temple is a lamp of encouragement and hope. It is a light of kindness and patience. Its light is a source of testimony and power. As God's people who are alive at this strategic moment in history, we have become the beautiful and intricate lampstand that sheds His light into dark and lonely places. As believers, we must be diligent and vigilant to ensure that our lives shine with His light and that it never fades regardless of the darkness surrounding us in this world.

> *And He has made us to be a kingdom, priests to His God and Father—to Him be the glory and the dominion forever and ever. Amen.*—Revelation 1:6

You have been given a job assignment by God the Father; your job is to act as a priest who forever presides over the light in His temple. God's house was never meant to be a place of darkness, murky living, or gloom, but because we are living on Earth as the representation of the tabernacle of His presence, the light of His presence should never subside or fade. Know your job and then do it! Shine as a vibrant demonstration of all that He has called you to be in Him!

A STRANGE PLACE

> *The Word became flesh, and dwelt among us.*—John 1:14

The word "dwelling" in this Scripture is the same word that is used for *"tabernacle"* in the Old Testament. God, in the Person of Jesus Christ, came to dwell, or to "tabernacle," among His people. The wilderness, in the Old Testament, was a very strange place for God to build His temple, and you, my friend, are a strange place, as well. Why would God choose us, broken pieces of humanity, to be the substance through which the light of His presence would shine?

The wilderness, of all places, is desperate for the glory and radiance of God. The wilderness of your ordinary, barren life is crying out for the luminous presence of God in the flesh. The wilderness of your ordinary, barren life is desperate for the grace of the mercy seat and the brilliance of the lampstand.

Only through you will the pure-gold experience of the mercy seat and the lampstand come to anyone's wilderness experience— only through you. If you refuse to bring His mercy and His light to the dry and dusty days of life, then the wilderness that surrounds you will remain hard and dark. Do not ignore the mercy seat of pure gold . . . it is a vital part of who you are! Never ignore the assignment of the lampstand of pure gold . . . it is a vital part of your calling in the Kingdom of God.

Do you not know that you are a temple of God and that the Spirit of God dwells in you? If any man destroys the temple of God, God will destroy him, for the temple of God is holy, and that is what you are.
—1 Corinthians 3:16–17

God has specific instructions concerning the building of His tabernacle, and we must come to Him on His exact terms. Your temple, which is your body and your very life, was always meant to be built precisely the way He designed in His Master Blueprint; His Master Blueprint is also known as the Bible.

Your life must contain a mercy seat and a lampstand. Those two items are what guarantee that you are living a life of pure gold significance in the eyes of God.

CHAPTER 13
FIRE EXTINGUISHERS

GOD PERPETUALLY AND ETERNALLY leads His children in a victory parade! God, who always has the last word, is marching His children toward an overwhelming conquest even when His dearly loved children are confronting a fire that was set by the enemy. However, in order to be led toward this God-directed victory, you must cooperate with God, lay down your opinions and preferences, and then boldly declare, "Lord, not my way, but Your way!"

God always wins, even when the fire of the enemy is attempting to destroy and permanently disable the life of a Christian. God takes the fire, which has been set by that miserable, old pyromaniac, the devil, and uses it to increase the fortitude and faith of His dearly loved children. God will work in us and with us until He wins!

God has created you to be a thermostat and not a thermometer. You were made to set the spiritual temperature not only of your life, but also of the world in which you live. You were not made to be burned by the fires of life or to allow difficult circumstances and events to raise your atmospheric temperature to a dangerous level.

The truth is that often we are burned by the fires in life and we feel unprepared and inadequate to control the raging temperatures of the blaze. However, there are some practical ways that God has provided in order to control the climate during your days on Earth. These practical disciplines will not only enable you to be a thermostat, but they will also help the fire do a cleansing work in your life so that you come out of the fire smelling like Jesus and not like smoke!

Part of the good that the Lord does in our lives through the process of the fire is to develop extinguishers that are especially able to lessen the temperature and to control the damage of a fire.

FASTING THROUGH THE FIRE

Esther was a young woman called by God to marry the king of Persia at a very difficult time in the history of this nation. Esther had been raised by her uncle, Mordecai, who was a righteous man; he deeply cared about the well-being of his niece. Uncle Mordecai offended Haman, the king's right-hand man, when he refused to bow to him at the city gate in spite of a royal ordinance. The overly sensitive and highly offended Haman then convinced King Ahasuerus to annihilate all of the Jews in the largest empire in the world. Esther, unbeknownst to the king, was of Jewish lineage and knew that she had been set in the palace for such a moment as this. Although her royal head was on the line, Esther did not shrink back, panic, or give in to the cruel demands of Haman.

Then Esther told them to reply to Mordecai, "Go, assemble all the Jews who are found in Susa, and fast for me; do not eat or drink for three days, night or day. I and my maidens also will fast in the same way. And thus I will go in to the king, which is not according to the law; and if I perish, I perish."—Esther 4:15–16

The choice to call a fast when facing a fire of gargantuan proportions enables a man or a woman to lay aside his or her own fear. Fasting also brings much-needed perspective to the wildfires of life, and it garners the attention of the best Firefighter of all time! When facing a fire, one can either press the panic button or choose to fast. Fasting always releases the anointing, favor, and blessing of God in the life of a believer. It also brings the breakthrough that is necessary for God's victorious plan to be established. The delivery room of every promotion and appointment is found in the powerful choice to fast one's way through a fire. When studying the Old Testament men and women who accomplished any type of significant work in the Kingdom of God, it can be observed that every single one of them chose to fast their way through a fire. Generally the fast was initiated during a time of transition or during a devastating challenge. If you long to make it through the fire with no residue of smoke on your life, then you will follow in the powerful footsteps of Esther, and you will call a fast in your life. Never underestimate the power of this fire extinguisher known as fasting; Esther saved an entire nation when she fasted for only three days. I wonder what damage has been done to my life by the heat of the fire simply because I refused to fast.

The word *"fast"* in the ancient Hebrew literally means "to close one's mouth." Biblical fasting can be simply stated as refraining from food for a spiritual purpose. One of the greatest delights of the fasting experience is that during the days of the chosen fast, one's spirit becomes uncluttered by the things of this temporary world. I have often wondered what breakthroughs I have missed in my life because I refused to fast. I have often wondered what victories I have aborted because I chose to eat rather than to close my mouth. I have often wondered what new assignments have been given to others because they chose to fast while I chose to eat. I refuse to be burned alive while shoving food in my mouth! I will fast and experience the refreshing and cooling presence of the Holy Spirit, even during the most hellacious days of my life.

FASTING GETS GOD'S ATTENTION

A desperate father approached Jesus and begged Him for mercy on his son, who was a lunatic. This heartbroken father, while on his knees, told Jesus the details of his son's life.

"Lord, have mercy on my son, for he is a lunatic and is very ill; for he often falls into the fire and often into the water. I brought him to Your disciples, and they could not cure him."—Matthew 17:15–16

Jesus knew that this boy could be cured and that His disciples needed to be taught an important lesson. Jesus simply rebuked the demon, and it immediately came out of the boy. The disciples were puzzled, and after the crowd had drifted away, they privately asked Jesus why they were unable to drive out the demonic spirit from the boy.

And He said to them, "Because of the littleness of your faith; for truly I say to you, if you have faith the size of a mustard seed, you will say to this mountain, 'Move from here to there,' and it will move; and nothing will be impossible to you. [But this kind does not go out except by prayer and fasting.]"—Matthew 17:20–21

Jesus knew that His disciples needed to understand the fact that fasting was the key to impossible situations. If you, like this desperate father, are facing an outrageously difficult circumstance, perhaps, like the disciples, you need to learn the value of the fast.

In a typical fast, a person generally will eliminate all foods for a given period of time, but will continue to drink large amounts of water. When going without food, it is of vital importance to raise one's intake of water and liquids. Some people choose to eliminate solid food, but they will continue to drink broth and juice. Novice fasters find it more feasible to initially eliminate only a food group, such as caffeine, sugar, or carbonated drinks. Some people choose to fast from television or from electronics.

If you are pregnant or have a serious medical condition, never go without food without a doctor's oversight. However, even if you are pregnant or are battling a long-term condition, you may still able to go without certain food groups, such as carbohydrates, sugar, or carbonated drinks, for a period of time.

The Daniel Fast, which is what I often commit to, eliminates meat, breads, and sweets. When Daniel chose to eat in this manner, his prayer was answered by the visitation of an angel and a breakthrough from Heaven. Fasting is always noticed by our Father, who sits on the throne. I believe that often He is waiting for me to show Him how serious I am concerning a breakthrough in my life by making the choice to fast.

Even Jesus, the most powerful and authoritative Man to ever live, chose to fast when He was in the wilderness of life. The choice of Jesus to fast at the beginning of His ministry established His position as more powerful than Satan.

If you are facing the fire right now, you need to fast. If you are in the wilderness today, you need to fast. If your world is falling apart, you need to fast. If you are battling with Satan, you need to fast. If your life is being threatened by disease, you need to fast. If you want breakthrough and promotion in your life, you need to fast!

Not only do the long-term effects of fasting set you in your God-ordained destiny, but fasting also has the miraculous power to lower the temperature of the fire.

FASTING BRINGS BREAKTHROUGH!

Just Joy! Ministries, the ministry I founded a decade ago, was struggling financially year after year after year. I knew that God had called me to help people live with joy according to the principles and practices found only in the Word of God. But it was becoming increasingly difficult to pay salaries, move the ministry ahead, and stay on the radio with the amount of money that was coming in. I began the year 2012 with a thirty-day fast. For twenty-five of the thirty days, I chose to follow the guidelines of a Daniel Fast, and then for five of the thirty days, I chose to drink liquids only.

The month of January passed with absolutely no change in the finances of the ministry; month after long month passed with absolutely no breakthrough and no change in the finances of the ministry. I knew that I had heard the voice of God calling me to fast for the ministry, and I stood in faith believing that God would make a way where there seemed to be no way.

On December 7, 2012, I had a dream that someone handed me a check for $10,000 on the very last day of the year. I told my husband, Craig, about my dream, as well as the CFO of the ministry, Angela Storm. I wanted them to know that I had heard from God and that He was still on His way with the miracle. Well, that didn't happen. No one gave me a check for $10,000 on December 31, 2012. However, a doctor friend who was in town asked Craig and me to meet him for breakfast on December 31, 2012. We met this powerful man of God and of medicine and had a wonderful time of sharing the Lord together. At the end of the breakfast, he handed me a New Year's card with my name on it and asked me to open it right there in the restaurant. In the envelope was a check for $50,000! It was the biggest gift that the ministry had ever received, and I believe that my decision to fast during the first thirty days of 2012 set the breakthrough in motion.

Fasting will always lower the temperature of the fire and will bring the miracle for which you have prayed!

THE COOLING EFFECTS OF WORSHIP

In this you greatly rejoice, even though now for a

little while, if necessary, you have been distressed by various trials, so that the proof of your faith, being more precious than gold which is perishable, even though tested by fire, may be found to result in praise and glory and honor at the revelation of Jesus Christ; and though you have not seen Him, you love Him, and though you do not see Him now, but believe in Him, you greatly rejoice with joy inexpressible and full of glory.—1 Peter 1:6–8

The strategic and powerful advice of Peter resounds through the centuries with an impact that will forever change the temperature of every fire you ever find yourself confronting. Peter challenges believers not only to *"rejoice"* but to *"greatly rejoice"*! This word *"greatly"* is a word that is peculiar to Christianity and was never used in the secular Greek. As Christians, we are the only ones who experience the thrill and fulfillment of "greatly" rejoicing. As twenty-first-century believers, we are the ones who singularly benefit from the command to "greatly" rejoice. As people who have been called to walk through the fire and not even smell like smoke, we are the only ones who are capable of benefiting from the choice to "greatly" rejoice! When a man or woman of God determines to "greatly" rejoice in the middle of suffering, this one influential determinant is able to lower the temperature of any Satan-set fire. This type of enthusiastic worship, in which Peter has called us to participate, remains unhindered and unrestricted by what is happening in the circumstances of our lives.

Rather than pitifully asking, "Why me?!" . . . we are a people who worship.

Rather than whining and weeping . . . we are a people who worship.

Rather than curl up in a fetal position and suck our emotional thumbs . . ., we are a people who worship!

The power of worship is that it places no importance or value on self or on self-comfort, but it places a singular focus on God, the Father of all that is good. Fires and the trials that fan them will not last forever, but our great worship should last into eternity.

So that the proof of your faith, being more precious than gold which is perishable, even though tested by fire, may be found to result in praise and glory and honor at the revelation of Jesus Christ.

When you embrace the challenge of Peter and elect to *"greatly rejoice,"* it is then that the proof of your faith, which is the most valuable commodity that you own, will give you an even greater reason to rejoice! Gold is the most valuable earthly commodity that exists; everything else that is judged to be of any value is compared to the current price of gold. Peter clearly states that your faith is more precious than gold to Jesus, even when gold is at its highest man-set price! Fire has the capacity of testing your faith, purifying your faith, and escalating the value of your faith. The fire will always rid your faith of self and make it more beautiful with the testing. Gold is not an eternal commodity, but your glorious faith will last forever!

And though you have not seen Him, you love Him, and though you do not see Him now, but believe in Him, you greatly rejoice with joy inexpressible and full of glory.

When all that you see around you are the fast-moving and destructive flames . . . what you love is Him!

When all you feel is the ferocious heat of a fire out of

control . . . what you believe is Him!

When the furnace is heated seven times hotter than it seems possible . . . you greatly rejoice!

We do not rejoice because of the fire or because of the trials, but we continue to greatly rejoice because of Him. It is only because of Him that we are able to rejoice *with joy inexpressible and full of glory!* The word *"inexpressible,"* which can also be translated *"indescribable,"* is used no other time in the New Testament. This word is endeavoring to portray a joy so deep and so profound that words do not hold the power to express it.

I know a pastor whose church in Florida holds a zip code in one of the most affluent regions in America. The people who attend his church have every material benefit they could ever desire and yet they still struggle with discouragement, purpose, and loneliness. This pastor decided to take a mission trip to Kenya just to escape for a short period of time the futility of pastoring a church of a materialistic mind-set. The people in Kenya have been through wars and famines, and many have lost members of their family, including children. However, the believers in Kenya are filled with joy inexpressible and full of glory. In spite of hunger and death, they sing their way through every day of their lives. These unspoiled, pure believers share the Word of God with one another while tears of joy are dripping down their faces. These Christians don't even know that they are living in the fire of great affliction, so pure are their hearts and so great is their joy. These men and women who live a world away from our lives of comfort and ease have discovered one of the greatest secrets imaginable this side of Heaven: Joy does not come from things or events . . . joy comes from Him!

The reason that we worship while in the fire is not because

we have it all . . . we worship because we have Him in spite of it all. We worship not because we have it all together . . . we worship because we have Him who holds it all together. We worship not because of what we are able to see in our circumstances . . . we worship because we have Him whom we do not see.

Sing Your Way Through the Fire

When our two oldest boys were in high school in North Carolina, we knew a family who lived on the other side of the city and who loved the Lord dearly. Their daughter, Karen, attended a Christian high school that our school often played against in sporting events. I enjoyed visiting with the mother of this delightful family as we shared many of the same values as we endeavored to raise our large families for Christ and His Kingdom. Karen was an athlete and a musician, and it was a delight to watch her grow up with a deep and abiding love for the Lord.

Early one Monday morning, just after our boys had left for school, I received a phone call from our principal, letting me know that Karen had been rushed to the hospital. She had gone to bed with a severe headache the night before and her mother had been unable to rouse her that morning. The principal was asking for prayer for this family, this mother, and this incredible daughter. Karen died forty-eight hours later due to a blood clot in her fourteen-year-old brain.

I went to Karen's funeral and sat near the back with my two sons, as well as some other families from the high school. The church had a one-thousand-seat sanctuary, and it was filled to overflowing with students, family, friends, neighbors, and coworkers. The largest group of people there were the teenagers. Kids who had played ball with Karen, young people who had gone to Sunday school with Karen, and others who had grown up in the same neighborhood with this amazing young lady were in attendance at her glorious memorial service. As her parents and siblings walked into the sanctuary, I couldn't help but sob along with every other mother in the standing-room-only auditorium.

The worship leader walked to the microphone with the joy of the Lord on his face and simply said, "Karen's parents have asked that you all join with them in singing a hymn of highest praise to the God who is always good. Will you sing with them, 'Great Is Thy Faithfulness'?"

And in that moment, Karen's parents stood to their feet, lifted their hands toward Heaven, and sang with joy inexpressible and full of glory:

"Great is Thy faithfulness, O God my Father!
There is no shadow of turning with Thee!
Thou changest not, Thy compassions they fail not,
Great is Thy faithfulness, Lord, unto me!"

Karen's parents knew the truth that you and I often ignore: Worship will always lower the temperature of a raging fire. Worship is what will usher you out of the fire unscathed, unharmed, and it is worship that will usher you out of the fire not even smelling like smoke.

CHAPTER 14

FIRE EXTINGUISHERS— TAKE TWO

ON MY KNEES

It was the last night that Jesus would ever live in freedom on the soil of Earth. He knew what was ahead of Him, and so He went to Gethsemane to pray. Peter, James, and John were the only disciples with Him this riveting evening, and He asked this trio of close friends to pray with Him and to pray for Him. Jesus desperately needed the prayer support of His three very best friends, and so He begged them to stay watchful in prayer.

Jesus walked over to a solitary location in the Garden of Gethsemane and fell on His face before the Father, crying, *"My Father, if it is possible, let this cup pass from Me; yet not as I will, but as You will"* (Matthew 26:39).

Jesus went back to His friends and found them sleeping during His deepest and darkest hour of need. Jesus looked at Peter, the one who had walked on water, and said, "Peter, could you not even stay awake for one hour and pray with Me?"

Jesus returned to the quiet place where He could pray without hearing the snores of his companions, and when He returned to where they were, once again, they were sound asleep. Jesus woke them up and begged them to please pray for Him.

Jesus then walked a distance away for the third time, and when He returned to those whom He loved, He found them asleep. These men who had seen Him feed the five thousand, raise Lazarus from the dead, turn water into wine, and calm an angry and violent storm were unable to even keep their eyes open when Jesus needed them the most.

It has always been interesting to me that in the Book of Matthew, only Peter's name is mentioned in this familiar and vital account of the time that Jesus spent in the Garden of Gethsemane. Jesus specifically asked Peter to stay awake and to pray at three different times. Peter, the man of strong opinion and vibrant personality, fell asleep three times and thus did not pray for Jesus. Peter mistakenly believed that he needed sleep more than he needed to pray.

Peter also denied Jesus three times. I wonder if Peter would have had the strength to faithfully witness for Jesus rather than deny Him if Peter had prayed rather than slept. Peter fell asleep three times . . . and Peter denied Jesus three times.

I wonder what I have sacrificed on the altar of sleep, or ego, or preference, when I should have been praying. I wonder if your life, or if my life would have turned out differently if we had prayed rather than slept . . . if we had prayed rather than watched TV . . . if we had prayed rather than shopped . . . if we had prayed rather than eaten . . . or if we had prayed rather than whined.

The story of Peter ricochets through the centuries and lands directly in our hands and in our hearts. We must pray so that we will remain strong and deeply committed to Christ in every challenge and temptation that comes our way.

BURNING COALS OF FIRE

Oftentimes, the most ferocious fires that are faced are the ones that are set by the incendiary practices of difficult people who burn and rage and ravage our otherwise peaceful and beatific lives. Is it possible to lessen the damage set by these ferocious, flame-bearing fiends? How is one able to deal with the wildfires of relationships and enemy crossfire?

"But I say to you, love your enemies and pray for those who persecute you."—Matthew 5:44

It always comes back to prayer, doesn't it? It always comes back to love and to prayer. If your life has been unfairly charred by flame-throwing people, the best possible choice that you can make is to love and to pray. Make a valiant effort and assertively love the difficult people in your life. You will be surprised at the refreshing joy that will follow simple acts of human kindness. Pray for the people who gossip about you, who abuse you, and who offend you. If all you do is throw fiery darts back at them, the fire will grow hotter and hotter, and you will find no relief in your life. But if you can determine to quench the heat of enemy fire with the cooling effects of prayer, your life will become a well-watered garden of God's blessing and of healthy relationships.

"But if your enemy is hungry, feed him, and if he is thirsty, give him a drink; for in so doing you will heap burning coals on his head."—Romans 12:20

This verse, found as a quotation written by the hand of one of the most persecuted men of all time, holds sound advice today for those of us who are dealing with difficult and contentious people. The advice is clear, well-stated, and holds immediate results. The question is, will you take Paul's advice or will you continue to play the blame game with those who have made your life a living hell?

Paul says to feed hungry enemies and to give a drink to enemies who are thirsty. In other words, take care of and provide for the wretched ones who thoughtlessly ravage your life. And what would be the result of this type of disarming behavior? *"For in so doing you will heap burning coals on his head."*

At initial glance, we might be tempted to rub our hot little hands together in glee and smugly declare, "Oh good! You gave it to me . . . now I'm going to give it to you! Get ready for some fire in your life, buddy!" But before you become immediately filled with vengeful glee, it is important to understand the background of the importance of burning coals.

Early every morning, while it was still dark and before the village was awake, the servants of a home or perhaps the older children would be sent to the center of town, where a fire had been burning all night long. On top of the head of the appointed person was a tin hat that was fashioned to hold burning coals from the village fire. The servant or child could scoop up the burning coals from the central fire and then place the tin hat back on their head as they walked back to their home. These burning coals would heat the family home during the day and would provide for the fire that would cook the food and cleanse the water that the family would drink that day. The burning coals would heat the water that would be used for bathing and for cleaning. The burning coals that one carried on his or her head were literally the provision for food, for water, and for cleanliness every day of the year.

When you are kind to someone who has been unkind, you are providing the valuable coals that will keep the offender alive and healthy. When you forgive someone who has offended you, you are giving a gift of life and safety to that despicable, yet loved piece of humanity.

When we offer "burning coals of fire" to a person who has brought only pain to our lives, we are giving to them the best kind of fire: a fire that warms, but does not destroy . . .

a fire that feeds, but does not ravage . . . a fire that provides for, but does not kill.

What a lovely advantage we have when we submit our lives to the call of the gospel! When our lives are guided and directed by the Bible, the fires that are set by our lives will never destroy, but will always edify.

PRAY AT ALL TIMES

> *"Truly I say to you, whoever says to this mountain, 'Be taken up and cast into the sea,' and does not doubt in his heart, but believes that what he says is going to happen, it will be granted him. Therefore I say to you, all things for which you pray and ask, believe that you have received them, and they will be granted you."*—Mark 11:23–24

When a flame-throwing, lava-spitting mountain stands in your way, this passage from the Gospel of Mark reveals the strategy that is needful. First of all, talk to the mountain! Tell the mountain to move and to be cast into the sea. Speaking to immovable mountains is one of the most fulfilling conversations that one can have this side of Heaven. However, talking to a mountain is not enough, because you must make sure that there is no doubt in your heart when you begin to boss mountains around! The words that you speak must be birthed from a place of absolute trust and faith. As you stare down that gargantuan and immovable mountain and begin to tell the mountain where to go, I have found that the most powerful declarations I can make are found in the Word of God.

> *"No weapon that is formed against me shall prosper."* (see Isaiah 54:17)

> *"And my God shall supply all of my needs according to His riches in glory."* (see Philippians 4:19)

"He pardons all my iniquities, He heals all my diseases." (see Psalm 103:3)

And we know that God causes all things to work together for good to those who love God, to those who are called according to His purpose.—Romans 8:28

The most powerful words you will ever speak to a mountain are the words found in Scripture. God, whose words caused the great rocks of mountains to tower over valleys and the plains, still has the authority in His Word to determine the location of mountains.

"Therefore, I say to you, all things for which you pray and ask, believe that you have received them, and they will be granted you."—Mark 11:24

After speaking to the towering mountains that block your progress in life, you must determine to talk to God. Prayer is simply a conversation between a person and God; it is a heartfelt exchange between a child and his or her Father. Prayer is, if nothing else, a conversation where a miracle is birthed. The potential power that is unleashed in prayer is most often experienced when the child repeats back to the Father the promises of His own heart. Prayer, then, becomes the same verbiage that was used in speaking to mountains.

"Father, You promised that I can do all things because You have given me Your strength."

"Father, Your Word says that it is not Your will that one should perish, so I ask You to save my son, in Jesus' name."

"Father, thank You for promising that You would never leave me nor forsake me."

SELF-SET INFERNOS

One of the most lethal fires that one can encounter is the fire that has been set by oneself. These self-set blazes often explode into murderous infernos by our choosing to wallow in sin and submitting to temptation. There is nothing that will destroy a life more efficiently and quickly than the choice to sin will do. Sin and compromise will melt the most beautiful of lives into a heap of indistinguishable ashes.

> *When He arrived at the place, He said to them, "Pray that you may not enter into temptation."*—Luke 22:40

Prayer is the most effective fire shield when used against the hot and destructive forces of sin and temptation. If the enemy is knocking at the door of your heart with continuous ideas of compromise, addictions, and sin, perhaps the words of Jesus are exactly what you need to obey. Prayer is able to give strength and a stubborn determination that no sin, no temptation, and no enemy is able to destroy.

> *"Therefore repent of this wickedness of yours, and pray the Lord that, if possible, the intention of your heart may be forgiven you."*—Acts 8:22

When your own choices have wickedly destroyed the landscape of your life, only the power of prayer is able to begin the healing and restorative work that you desperately need. When sin and compromise have led you directly into harm's way and you find yourself surrounded by the purgatory of evil and its twin sister, disobedience, it is prayer that will usher in a cooling shower of forgiveness and God's presence.

> *In the same way the Spirit also helps our weakness; for we do not know how to pray as we should, but the Spirit Himself intercedes for us with groanings too deep for words.*—Romans 8:26

If the flames of mass destruction have closed every possible way of escape, pray that the Holy Spirit will pray through you! The thoughts and words of the Holy Spirit are able to immediately make a way where there seems to be no way. The heart and power of the Holy Spirit contain the healing salve of Heaven in their very essence, so cry out boldly, *"Holy Spirit! Pray through me right now!"*

CHAPTER 15

AND IF THAT WASN'T ENOUGH . . .

A N INORDINATE NUMBER OF THE FIRES that we encounter in life are set by the choices of other people. There are blazes set by gossipers, bonfires set by dysfunctional family members, flames that are stirred up by jealous coworkers, and the holocaust instigated by strangers. The fires that are birthed in human relationships are the most difficult to put out and can cause blistering, searing pain that create hurtful damage long after the flames have been stifled.

Interpersonal fires need more than human intervention; interpersonal fires need the expert advice and cooling strategy of Jesus Christ. Often it is impossible to deal with these particular fires without divine intervention and without showers of blessing from the water towers of heaven.

"But I say to you who hear, love your enemies, do good to those who hate you, bless those who curse you, pray for those who mistreat you."—Luke 6:27–28

And there you have it. It is God's solution to Earth's injustice. Therein lies the heart of the Father toward His quibbling, angry, bellicose offspring.

Love. Do good. Bless. Pray. Could it be any simpler than that?

YOU CAN LOVE

What does it mean to love someone who has wronged you so vehemently that a roaring fire breaks out instinctively? Is it even possible to love a noxious, hateful, cantankerous person?

It must be possible, or Jesus would not have asked us to do it. What is true is that I am unable to love difficult people without the love of the Father flowing through me, and so once again I find myself at His feet begging for more—begging for more strength . . . for more power . . . for more love . . . for more of Him and less of me.

Love often begins in small ways. A smile can cool a roaring inferno. Love can be initiated in the simplest of words: "*I'm sorry*." Often the most loving choice you or I can make is to walk away from the diatribe of angry words and refuse to be involved in the volatile disagreement.

Jesus doesn't want you to be abused . . . He just wants you to be unselfish. If you are in an abusive relationship, get out and get help. However, if your fiery furnace has been set, not by an abuser but by an accuser, you can choose to love even when your flesh cries out in pain.

Loving a difficult person can be challenging, but it is possible. One of the hardest challenges that presents itself on Earth is to be kind to cruel people. Only through Christ and in Christ are we able to love truly unlovable human beings.

Can you smile? Can you say, "I'm sorry"? Can you make a coffee date? Can you bake a loaf of bread? Can you make a meal? Can you buy a gift? Can you listen?

If you answered, "Yes, of course I can," to any of these questions, then you can love.

YOU CAN DO GOOD

My husband and I found ourselves in a volatile and hateful church situation many years ago. There were misunderstandings on both sides, and the accusations were growing out of control toward us. Craig and I purposed four things in our hearts during that time.

1 – We would choose joy.
2 – We would refuse to gossip.
3 – We would believe the best.
4 – We would walk in victory and hope.

The most demanding and strenuous item on that list was the determination not to gossip. While our name was being slung through the mud, we did not defend ourselves. When the untruths spoken about us served as dry and brittle kindling to the fire that was being set, we refused to retaliate. The Word of God instructed us to "*do good to those who hate you,*" and so not only did we not gossip, but then we began to speak words of love and blessing about those who were destroying our reputation.

The fire began to die down, and the damage seemed to be under control. God was working a miracle in the situation because we chose to do good to those who disliked us. The situation is still not perfect, but it is certainly not as hot nor is it as destructive as it used to be.

YOU CAN BLESS

As children of God, not only must we refuse gossip and speaking an evil report when others are setting fire to our lives, but we must determine to bless those pyromaniacs with our words and with our actions. The fire will go out much more quickly and the damage will be significantly less severe when a person makes the defiant choice to verbally bless and therefore encourage the offender. When you choose to deal with the fires set by others with God's wisdom and advice, you will be the beneficiary of a cooling breeze from heaven and the luscious aroma of His very presence. When you resist gossip and negativity and instead embrace blessing and encouragement, the fire will miraculously die down and diminish in strength. Choosing to engage in vengeful and oftentimes justifiable slander will fan the flames of the inferno, but when one chooses to speak words of benevolence and comfort, God will send showers of blessing that will immediately quench the searing heat.

YOU CAN PRAY

It always comes back to prayer, doesn't it? Every situation that is faced in life can be solved with a commitment to spend more time on our knees talking to God about it than we do in talking to others about it. The miracle that happens in prayer is that not only does God hear us, but our hearts are changed due to the time spent with the Father, who is the greatest Firefighter of all!

Prayer is a position of power and purpose when dealing with the unnecessary and cruel fires instigated by difficult people. You will find, while on your knees, that God's presence is the only protection that you need when in this particular furnace. You will find, while on your knees, that God truly does have the best advice. You will find, while on your knees, that He is more than enough to guide you through the smoke and flames.

YOU CAN LEARN

"Whoever hits you on the cheek, offer him the other also; and whoever takes away your coat, do not withhold your shirt from him either. Give to everyone who asks of you, and whoever takes away what is yours, do not demand it back. Treat others the same way you want them to treat you."—Luke 6:29–31

The call of Heaven has not changed in over two thousand years since Jesus spoke these words to broken people. It is not enough to merely choose not to retaliate, but one must go beyond pacifism to bestowing a conscious and audible blessing. I have found power in treating others not just the way that I want to be treated, but in choosing to treat others the way I would want them to treat my own children. There is something about a mother's heart that rises up in great pain and indignation whenever one of her precious children is mistreated. I have decided that the call of God on my life is to treat everyone I come in contact with the same way I desire that others treat my five incredible kids!

WHAT CREDIT IS THAT TO YOU?

"If you love those who love you, what credit is that to you? For even sinners love those who love them. If you do good to those who do good to you, what credit is that to you? For even sinners do the same. If you lend to those from whom you expect to receive, what credit is that to you? Even sinners lend to sinners in order to receive back the same amount. But love your enemies, and do good, and lend, expecting nothing in return; and your reward will be great, and you will be sons of the Most High; for He Himself is kind to ungrateful and evil men. Be merciful, just as your Father is merciful."—Luke 6:32–36

As men and women of God, it is of utmost importance that our standard of living and rules of behavior are in submission to the principles found in the Bible. The world and its counsel are worthless in the life of someone who honors Jesus Christ. When dealing with difficult people and fractious relationships, continually remind yourself that the Word is true and the world is incorrect. There is not a person who has ever lived who has a better idea than the Bible or who is able to contribute advice to the Lord. If the family of God sincerely put into practice the counsel of the wisdom of God, there would be far fewer dysfunctional families, divorces, and Hatfield versus McCoy–type battles!

The truth is that all families are dysfunctional in some manner; however, functional families handle their dysfunction in a functional and healing manner.

> *"Do not judge, and you will not be judged; and do not condemn, and you will not be condemned; pardon, and you will be pardoned. Give, and it will be given to you. They will pour into your lap a good measure— pressed down, shaken together, and running over. For by your standard of measure it will be measured to you in return."*—Luke 6:37–38

These verses apply directly to our relationships with the most difficult and belligerent people in life. Often we have singularly used, *"Give, and it shall be given to you. They will pour into your lap a good measure—pressed down, shaken together, and running over. For by your standard of measure it will be measured to you in return,"* as specifically applying to finances. However, when read in the context of what Jesus was teaching, it becomes obviously apparent that the primary meaning of these words was meant to be applied to relationships with those who are fractious and disagreeable. This is a promise found nestled in the words of the New Testament: When a believer refuses to judge, others will find it nearly impossible to judge the life that guile-free believer! When a Christian refuses to condemn others, it will be extremely difficult to find a reason or a source of condemnation in that pure Christian's life! When a man or a woman determines to be the first to forgive, forgiveness will easily be given to them. Not only will this powerful believer be free from the pain of others' judgment, condemnation, and bitterness, but this extraordinary Christian will be given a blessing that is unable to be measured or controlled!

CHAPTER 16
THE WORD . . . THE WORD . . . THE WORD

MANY CHRISTIANS, when encountering a fire, lay their Bibles aside and then justify this poor decision with excuses such as, *"I am too depressed to read my Bible . . . I am too weary to read the Word of God . . . I am too traumatized to open the Bible . . . God understands why I can't read the Bible right now."*

It is precisely because of the fiery trial and the trauma of its blaze that it is absolutely imperative to read the Word of God! When the fires are raging and the heat is at an all-time high, the Bible can do for you what absolutely nothing else and no one else has the power to accomplish in your life. You need to read the Bible, because it has the potential to bring much-needed comfort during days of great tragedy. The Word of God is more vital than friendship, finances, or other creature comforts when one's world is absolutely falling apart.

Before the written Word of God came into existence, God often spoke to men and women in visions and dreams, as well as with His audible voice. Today, one can simply open the Bible to a beloved psalm, a comforting verse from the Book of John, or a Holy Spirit–inspired thought from Paul to hear the voice of the Lord. God is still speaking today, and when He speaks it always confirms the written Word of God. The Bible is God's heart and God's thoughts given to humankind. When God speaks today, it never contradicts the written Word, nor does it set different boundaries from those that have been presented from Genesis to Revelation.

There is a long-term, even eternal benefit that occurs when

a believer chooses to read the Bible and listen to the voice of God during challenging times. God's Word is able to quench the fire and lessen the long-term effects of the fire.

ABRAM AND GOD

Abram and his wife, Sarai, had lived in the fire of infertility and dashed hopes for decade after decade of their married life. Abram had obeyed God through the challenge of transition and had even generously given to his nephew, Lot, the very best of the land. God had promised Abram that He would bless him and make him into a great nation.

But, God, Abram may have thought, *where are the babies? Where is the blessing? Where is the fulfillment of Your promise to me?*

Abram was sorely downcast, and his heart was broken because he wanted more from life than he had been given. Abram wanted more than empty promises. When Abram was in this emotionally destitute condition, he made the very foolish decision to play *"Let's Make a Deal"* with God. This decision never turns out well! I would never recommend anyone attempt to play this ridiculous game with the Creator of all that is good. Let's listen in to this riveting conversation that God had with the discouraged and brokenhearted Abram:

> *After these things the word of the Lord came to Abram in a vision, saying, "Do not fear, Abram, I am a shield to you; your reward shall be very great."*—Genesis 15:1

The power in the Word of the Lord is that it always confronts the fear issues hidden in the heart of a man or a woman. The Word of God will confront and then assuage your fear of failure, fear of the future, fear of sickness, and fear of lack. The Word of God has the supernatural power to comfort a discouraged and broken heart and then to banish all remnants of fear and worry. If a fearful person refuses to read the Bible, his or her fear of the unknown will exponentially grow and then be impossible to avoid or to conquer.

However, the Word of God will always remind you who God is and what His promises are. To Abram, the Word of the Lord came to abolish his fear and to remind him that God was able to protect him from harm and disappointment. In this verse, God also reiterated the promise that there was a covenant blessing on the way from Heaven toward Abram's infertile life. Abram was about to be the beneficiary of a great reward, because the Word of the Lord had declared it!

Whenever a believer finds himself as an object of the fiery darts of the enemy, the foremost thing that comes to their mind should not be fear, but it should be the promises and the presence of God. Rather than rehearsing and marinating in all that is wrong with life, perhaps a better idea is to remember all of the promises of our great God! Especially when confronting a fire, it is of vital importance to think about and then to talk about the goodness and the promises of God, regardless of the barren and charred landscape that a fire has caused. You may only see devastation with your natural eye, but your spiritual eye should remain focused on and captured by the panorama of the promises and faithfulness of God. If you are not in the Word of God, the enemy will try to victimize you with spiritual amnesia, which will cause you to forget all of the great promises that God has made toward you!

Abram said, "O Lord God, what will You give me, since I am childless, and the heir of my house is Eliezer of Damascus?"—Genesis 15:2

Abram, as a victim of the fire of disappointment, was all bound up in "I," "me," and "mine." This is navel-gazing at its most inappropriate, and Abram was only capable of talking about his human pain and of his indignation at God.

In eavesdropping on this conversation that the man Abram was having with the God of the universe, I always want to interrupt and exclaim, "Take it back, Abram! You don't mean that! Just stop talking, Abram, and listen to God!"

Then I humbly wonder if the Holy Spirit has ever wanted to interrupt my conversations with God and say, "Stop, Carol! You don't mean that! Just stop talking and listen to the Lord who loves you and is working all things together for your good!"

Times of testing will either bring out the worst in you or the best in you; you will either focus on self or you will focus on God. The fire will cause a person to either think about everything that has been denied to them, or they will meditate on the glorious and sure promises of God the Father.

In this exchange between a man and his God, Abram said to the Lord, *"What will You give me, since I am childless . . ."* Abram was fixated on what he did not have rather than on whom he was with! It is in the fire that one's focus is of primary importance. You can either focus on lack, or you can focus on the bounty and the provision of Jehovah-Jireh, your Provider. The Word of God must take the front-and-center place in your life when confronting a fire, because the Word will enable you to focus wholeheartedly on who God is. Abram's mistake was focusing on self and on what he was lacking, which is precisely why this discouraged man needed to hear the voice of God. That is why you and I need to hear God's voice, as well. God's Word will enable a person to get his or her eyes off of self and away from their personal lack; God's Word will enable a person to focus on who God is during times of affliction and challenge.

And Abram said, "Since You have given no offspring to me, one born in my house is my heir."—Genesis 15:3

Poor Abram! Poor God to have to engage in a conversation with an ungrateful, blaming man! This conversation is going nowhere fast! God had specifically come to Abram in a vision to encourage this man, and yet all that Abram could do was murmur, complain, and blame. Do you see yourself in this story yet? God intends for every encounter with Him and with His Word to encourage a person in their moment of pain. However, when a pessimistic, dispirited person insists on blaming God, he or she is missing the blessing that an encounter with God is able to bring!

This time of waiting had certainly brought out the very worst in Abram, and he chose to blame God for all of his problems and for his lack. *"Since You have given no offspring to me,"* starkly reveals the level of blame in Abram's heart toward the God of all comfort and mercy.

When God makes a promise, generally what follows that promise is a time of waiting. What you choose to do during this waiting period and what you choose to say during this time of perceived delay reveals what is in your heart toward the Father. We all must wait for something, so purpose in your heart to wait well. Waiting poorly encompasses whining, sinful actions or blaming God; waiting well always includes worship, trust, and powerful declarations.

Then behold, the word of the Lord came to him, saying, "This man will not be your heir; but one who will come forth from your own body, he shall be your heir."—Genesis 15:4

The Word of the Lord is able to clarify emotions and perceived circumstances in a powerful and resounding way!

It is of great necessity not to process human pain through circumstances or events, but only through the promises found in the Word of God. And you, my friend, need to read your Bible if you desire to hear the voice of the Lord and be exposed to the Word of the Lord. God speaks through other venues and other disciplines, but it is by reading the Bible on a consistent basis that you will be able to fully participate in the luxury of hearing the voice of God. God also speaks through the lyrics of the great hymns of the faith and through the words of worship choruses and songs. God often speaks through Christian literature and through sermons and teachings. However, it is through the words found in the Bible that God speaks most powerfully and most lucidly. Also, it is absolutely true that when you are reading the Bible as a personal discipline, it opens your spiritual ears to hear His voice from those other venues more clearly.

FROM COMPLAINING TO COUNTING!

And He took him outside and said, "Now look toward the heavens, and count the stars, if you are able to count them." And He said to him, "So shall your descendants be."
—Genesis 15:5

The Word of the Lord takes you out of the small place of your own selfish choosing and miraculously sets you in a larger place of God's appointment. The Word of the Lord exchanges your human perspective for God's divine and eternal perspective. God is insistent upon taking His children out of their place of pain and blame and placing us in situations where we are able to look up at what God is able to do! God's perspective will never agree with your blame game. We have heard Abram talking about self, about disappointments, and about casting blame, but God was saying, "Hey, Abe! Let's count the stars together!"

When we insist on playing *Let's Make a Deal* with God or the blame game with others, God always says, "I have a better idea than that! *Let's Count the Stars Together!*"

What God has planned for your life is so magnificent and awe-inspiring that in your human abilities you will never be able to comprehend it. God said to Abram, *"Count the stars, if you are able to count them."* Why, of course Abram was unable to count the stars of the universe, but God could! You are unable to fathom all that God has planned for your life, but God is able to dream infinitely bigger dreams than anything you could ever come up with on your own. Not only must we listen to the God who is able to count the stars, but we must trust the God who counts the stars. Trusting God includes having absolute trust and faith in His chosen timetable. If God promised something, it will come to pass in His time.

> *Then he believed in the Lord; and He reckoned it to him as righteousness.*—Genesis 15:6

The Word of the Lord will always lead you away from a place of pain and blame, and then lead you toward a place of trust and belief in the God of Creation. Abram had an "aha" moment when he listened to what God had been trying to tell him all along. The Word of God will challenge your doubts and will boldly lead you into agreement with God's opinion.

Perhaps this is what the time of waiting has been all about in the life of Abram. Perhaps God was intent on capturing Abram's heart and aligning it with God's own heart. While we wait, we must not lean in to our own understanding, but trust the God who delights in counting the stars!

You and God

> *You also become imitators of us and of the Lord, having received the word in much tribulation with the joy of the Holy Spirit.*—1 Thessalonians 1:6

If you love nothing else about this book . . . you must love the power and the life-changing truth that is in this one, single verse found nestled in the Book of 1 Thessalonians! When going through a tribulation or a fire in life, you need the Word of God more than you need water to drink or air to breathe. The Word of God is able to change days of tribulation into sweet moments of joy because of the power of the Holy Spirit. The Bible will give you the joy to carry on during days that would, in the natural, be suffocating and crushing. The Word of God is miraculous, and it is able to do a miracle in you. When life is filled with mind-boggling sufferings, His Word can infuse a supernatural joy into your life!

"Margie" suffered a crushing mental breakdown when she was only in her mid-thirties. The stress of life had become overwhelming, between trying to raise three children, be a loving wife, work a full-time job, care for an aging mother, and stay active in her local church. One day, she just couldn't do it anymore, and Margie experienced a full and explosive breakdown in front of her entire family. Margie spent three weeks in the mental ward at the finest hospital in the region. The doctors kept her sedated, and as the weeks rolled by, her husband wondered if he would ever again get to embrace and converse with the woman whom he loved more than life itself. Margie's husband one night asked the doctors to diminish the amount of drugs that they were putting in her system, and he began to read the Word of God over her. This incredible husband and father worked all day, came home and fixed a quick meal for his children, and then went to the hospital and sat by her bed for hours into every night. Every minute that he was sitting by her bed, he read to his sweet wife from the Bible. Margie, to this day, decades later, remembers that it was the Word of God that brought her back to sanity. She began not only to be cognizant of what her husband was reading to her from the Bible, but she also began to recall Scriptures that she had memorized as a child in Sunday school. Margie's emotions and mental challenges were healed by the power of the Bible. Margie never again struggled emotionally or mentally and has spent the five decades following the nervous breakdown teaching other women the power and stability that is found in the Word of God.

The Word of God is able to give to you what people are unable to give. The Bible will strengthen you in ways that the gym or the finest personal trainer is unable to strengthen you. The holy Scriptures will supply you with answers that mere book learning is unable to supply. The Bible is miraculously equipped to bring joy in dark and foreboding circumstances and to usher in peace when all around is confusion.

A DEADLY WEAPON

And take the helmet of salvation, and the sword of the Spirit, which is the word of God.—Ephesians 6:17

When Paul penned these words by the inspiration of the Holy Spirit, he was well-acquainted with the weapons of warfare that Roman soldiers employed. There were several different types of swords used by the finest fighting battalion at that time in history. Paul did not use general words in his verbiage, but he described a very specific type of sword. Not only would Paul have been familiar with the different types of swords utilized by the Roman army, but an average citizen alive at this time in history would know the differences found in the swords, as well.

The *gladius* sword was an extremely heavy sword with an unusually long blade, and it was the most beautiful of all of the Roman swords. However, the *gladius* sword was also known to be cumbersome and awkward and was known as a two-handed sword due to the fact that a Roman soldier had to use two hands to swing it. The *gladius* sword was sharpened only on one side, with the opposing side being only blunt and dull. If a soldier were to swing the *gladius* sword at an approaching opponent, the enemy would most likely only be bruised and not killed. The word that Paul uses for "sword" in Ephesians 6:17 is not the word *gladius* but a more specific version of the ancient Roman sword.

Roman soldiers often used daggers as vital components of their weapons of warfare. This was a shorter sword, and soldiers hid them somewhere in their uniforms. However, it was hard to get out in times of battle. The dagger is not the sword that Paul refers to in Ephesians 6:17.

Machaira is the specific type of sword that Paul is referencing in this verse in Ephesians. The *machaira* sword was a brutal weapon of murder, about nineteen inches long. Both sides of the blade were razor-sharp, and this particular sword was more dangerous and lethal than all other swords that a Roman soldier might have in his employ. The tip of the *machaira* sword turned upward, with an extremely sharp and deadly point. The *machaira* sword inflicted the very worst type of wound, which was often lethal. When a Roman soldier had the opportunity to thrust a *machaira* sword into the gut of an enemy soldier, he would hold the sword very tightly with both hands and then give it a wrenching twist inside the enemy's stomach. The entrails of his enemy spilled out as the valiant Roman soldier yanked the *machaira* from the enemy's torso.

Before you gulp in revulsion and cry out, *"Too much information! Why did I need to know that?"* let me explain to you exactly why this detailed information is important today as we fight the flinger of the fiery darts. This description of the capability of the *machaira* sword is exactly what the

Bible says the Word of God is able to do when used against the enemy. The *machaira* sword was the most dangerous of all known swords, and the Bible is the most lethal force one can ever utilize against the forces of the enemy. The dreaded *machaira* sword was intended not only to kill an opponent in battle but to completely rip an enemy's internal organs to shreds. No enemy who encountered the vicious point of the *machaira* sword lived to tell about it.

Paul, in this verse in Ephesians, was declaring that God has provided a weapon that is brutal and murderous when used against the enemy. This singular weapon, the sword of the Spirit, which is the Word of God, will absolutely rip your enemy to shreds! The *machaira* sword inevitably left an enemy lying on the ground in a puddle of blood, never to get up again. This particular enemy that had just felt the devastating effects of the *machaira* sword would never be able to come back as the bearer of a *machaira* sword again. The Holy Spirit, through the writings of Paul, instructs that the Word of God is like the deadly *machaira* sword; it will do terrible and final damage to the enemy aggressor who lives to set fires in your life.

TWO-MOUTHED SWORD

The Holy Spirit, through the writings of Paul in the Book of Ephesians, gives one other detail concerning the deadly *machaira* sword. Although many translations describe this sword as "two-edged," the correct translation is actually a "two-mouthed" sword. The Greek word *distomos*, which is used to describe the *machaira* sword, should not be translated as "two-edged," but rather as "two-mouthed." The reason that this detail is of profound importance is that for the Word of God to do its victorious work, it first must come out of His mouth, which it has, and then it must come out of *your* mouth! The strategy that enables you to brandish the power in the Word of God is to speak it audibly. You must declare the Word of God for it to do its fighting and powerful work.

This is why it is vital for you to have a daily quiet time and to go to a weekly Bible Study. This explains why it is necessary for you to talk about the Word of God with friends and go to a church where the Bible is preached. You must be prepared, so that when the enemy comes at you full-force (and he will!), you will have something to respond with! If you stop short of confessing or declaring the Word of God, then sadly you are stopping one step short of complete and total victory. It is not enough just to *think* the Word of God—you must *declare* the Word of God!

A HEALING WORK

And then, Hebrews 4:12, brings to a fulfilling conclusion not only what the Word of God is able to do to an enemy aggressor, but also what the Word is able to do in you: *"piercing even to the dividing asunder of soul and spirit, and of the joints and marrow, and is a discerner of the thoughts and intents of the heart."*

Not only does the Bible have the focused power to do a destructive work in the enemy, but it also has the power to do a healing and revealing work in the hearts of God's children. When we study and meditate on God's Word, it is able to miraculously cut through the muck and the mire of our mind and our emotions. The Word of God is able to go to the heart of the matter and separate the good from the bad, the healthy from the sick, and the truth from the lie. The Word has spiritual eyes and is able to see or discern exactly what is going on in our hearts. The Bible is able to see what our human eyes are unable to see. Once the Word of God is placed in the heart of a believer, it instantly goes to work to renovate areas in our lives that are unbalanced or unhealthy. The Bible is able to do a renovation and a remodeling on all that is wounded and scurrilous in each one of us.

If we are foolish and shortsighted enough to ignore the Word of God, old patterns of wrong thinking and bondages from the past will continue to have full sway in our lives. However, meditating on the Word of God will assuredly release a healing operation of heavenly proportions in our lives. The Word of God acts like a surgeon's scalpel and goes to the heart of the diseased matter in us. The Word is able to do what no spouse, no friend, no counselor, no pastor, no teacher, no psychologist, no doctor, and no psychiatrist is able to do. The Bible has the miraculous power to divide between one's soul and one's spirit, and then it discerns the thoughts and the human intentions of one's heart. When we allow the Word to do this extraordinary work in us, we are inwardly changed and forever healed. When the Word of God does its healing and revealing work in us, we then become stronger and lovelier than ever before. The Word enables us to become what we are unable of becoming in our own human strength. The eternal treasure, which is found only in the Bible, calls forth the person whom Heaven has always intended for you to be.

So faith comes from hearing, and hearing by the word of Christ.—Romans 10:17

This is the final installation in an incredible series of events! When you declare the Word of God over the enemy who has set the horrific fires in your life, he is rendered senseless and useless. Then the Word of God does a healing work inside of you and removes the gunk and germs of unhealthy emotions and sick thinking. Then you become a believer of gargantuan and immovable faith!

Never underestimate the importance of studying, meditating

on, and praying the Word of God. When you choose to study, meditate on, and pray the Word of God, it miraculously becomes a literal and integral part of who you are. The next time you face a firestorm or find yourself spending time in a fiery furnace, the very first thought that crosses your mind should be from the Word of God! The very first word that comes out of your mouth, when encountering the roar of the flames, should be from the Word of God! Nothing else will ever do!

CHAPTER 17
BACK TO THE WILDERNESS

JESUS HAD JUST BEEN BAPTIZED by John the Baptist and had heard His Father's heavenly voice declaring over His life, *"This is My beloved Son, in whom I am well-pleased"* (Matthew 3:17).

After this magnificent experience at the Jordan River, Jesus was not led into ministry, nor into performing miracles; He did not go to the Temple to preach, nor did He feed thousands of hungry people. At this juncture in His earthly ministry, Jesus was led by the Holy Spirit into the wilderness to be tempted by the devil. Jesus and the devil were not strangers to one another, but their lives had collided thousands of times throughout the history of God's children. Jesus had been there in eternity past when Satan took one-third of the heavenly host in a rebellion against God. Jesus had seen the great conflict and heard the final resolution as God had thrown the deceiver down to Earth.

Now, Jesus, the Man, would confront the evil of the ages in a wilderness battle that had the power and impact to ricochet throughout history. How would Jesus, completely God and yet completely man, fight the lying, deceiving, cheating, and evil entity known as Satan? What weapons would He utilize in the greatest confrontation of good versus evil since the world had been created?

Then Jesus was led up by the Spirit into the wilderness to be tempted by the devil. And after He had fasted forty days and forty nights, He then became hungry. And the tempter came and said to Him, "If You are the Son of God, command that these stones become bread." But He answered and said, "It is written, 'Man shall not live on bread alone, but on every word that proceeds out of the mouth of God."—Matthew 4:1–4

Jesus faced the enemy the exact same way that you and I should face him: Jesus declared in this mad demon's face, "It is written!" When Jesus desired to use a two-mouthed sword against the accuser of the brethren and the father of all lies, He drew it out, used it, and *twisted* it!

Then the devil took Him into the holy city and had Him stand on the pinnacle of the temple, and said to Him, "If You are the Son of God, throw Yourself down; for it is written, 'He will command His angels concerning You'; and 'On their hands they will bear You up, so that You will not strike Your foot against a stone.'" Jesus said to him, "On the other hand, it is written, 'You shall not put the Lord your God to the test.'"—Matthew 4:5–7

The enemy reasoned in his despotic, infested heart that he could use the Word of God just as well as Jesus was able to use it, and so Satan quoted the Word of God out of context and with an evil mind-set. When the enemy chose to try to engage the Word in his battle, Jesus came back with a Scripture and quoted it correctly, truthfully, and boldly.

The Word of God ought to be in you, my friend, just like it was in Jesus at the moment of His fiercest battle. It is of vital importance that the Word of God is not mere head knowledge, but that it becomes heart knowledge for you and therefore an active principle in your life. The devil knew the Word, but he only knew it as head knowledge. You and I, as children of the Most High God, must place the Word of God deeply within us, so that when we are engaged in warfare with the father of all lies, we are able to effectively and powerfully declare the truth that is found only in the Word.

Again, the devil took Him to a very high mountain and showed Him all the kingdoms of the world and their glory; and he said to Him, "All these things I will give You, if You fall down and worship me." Then Jesus said to him, "Go, Satan! For it is written, 'You shall worship the Lord your God, and serve Him only.'" Then the devil left Him; and behold, angels came and began to minister to Him.—Matthew 4:8–11

When the Word of God was applied for the third time to the monstrous lies of the enemy, he whimpered in embarrassing surrender, tucked his broken tail between his scrawny legs, and slithered off to feel sorry for himself. The deceiver of the brethren dashed away in utter and total defeat. He who had been so braggadocios only moments before knew that he was in a losing battle against the absolute authority of the Word of God. The Bible will always have the last Word . . . the final Word . . . the authoritative Word . . . the winning Word . . . and the triumphant Word!

FINALLY

If you have found yourself under enemy attack, and if you have found yourself surrounded by a ferocious fire raging around you, ask God to give you a Scripture with which to fight. When you discern your battle verse, stand on it . . . declare it . . . and pray it! The enemy is unable to stand and continue to fight when one of God's children fights in the same manner that Jesus fought when confronted by Satan in the wilderness.

One of the most amazing and defining results that fighting the enemy's fire with the Word of God produces is that not only will you exit the fire without being charred or destroyed, but you will indeed come out of the fire stronger and bolder then when you first experienced the blistering flames of the

143

fire. You will come out of the fire as the very best version of you and as a force to be reckoned with in the Kingdom and purposes of God. The fire has the capacity of becoming your finest hour when you battle the searing, scorching flames of the fire with the power that is only found in the Word of God. The fire is actually the mighty springboard that God is able to use to propel a believer into his or her destiny when the believer adheres to the firefighting techniques of divine instructions.

CHAPTER 18
ARSONISTS AND PYROMANIACS

THE FIRES OF LIFE possess the singular capacity to take what is ordinary, cheap, and unauthentic, and turn that very substance into pure gold. The heat removes the dross and impurities of the heart and it also enables God, the Silversmith, to see His glorious reflection in a human life. Men and women who embrace the process of the fire are miraculously able to reflect the face of Jesus.

There are different types of fires that are encountered in life; some fires are set by circumstances out of your control, while other fires are ignited by personal choices. The most difficult type of fire to encounter is the brand of fire that has been set by another person.

YOUR GOAL

For this finds favor, if for the sake of conscience toward God a person bears up under sorrows when suffering unjustly. For what credit is there if, when you sin and are harshly treated, you endure it with patience? But if when you do what is right and suffer for it you patiently endure it, this finds favor with God. For you have been called for this purpose, since Christ also suffered for you, leaving you an example for you to follow in His steps, who committed no sin, nor was any deceit found in His mouth; and while being reviled, He did not revile in return; while suffering, He uttered no threats, but kept entrusting Himself to Him who judges righteously.—1 Peter 2:19–23

The Holy Spirit, through the pen of the great man of faith Peter, is teaching Christians from all generations exactly how to deal with difficult relationships in life. Peter, who had rebuked the Lord and later cut off the ear of an advancing soldier, had learned from the example of Christ how to deal with contentious and ornery people. In these verses, Peter is exhorting us to act like Jesus and not like Peter. Peter, after being filled with the Holy Spirit, had learned how to respond to those who chose to mistreat God's beloved children.

When you experience harsh treatment and even suffering due to the words and actions of the people in your life, there is a way to extract God's favor from that unfair and difficult situation. The result of being kind to unkind people, forgiving difficult people, and serving others who have only been cruel to you is worthy of a blessing so rich and rare that it captures the heart of God Himself. God responds to those who have chosen to be kind to ornery and fractious people by showering His loving favor into their deserving lives. The Holy Spirit and Peter agree on this powerful principle discovered by observing the life of Christ: It is important to patiently endure suffering that is rendered by cruel people.

"Patiently enduring suffering" includes refusing to gossip, not feeling compelled to tell your side of the difficult story, and then continuing to walk ahead with joy and peace. Do not allow the culture of Oprah and "It's All About Me!" to dictate how you are allowed to act while others are mistreating you. We must handle people-fires the way that the Bible instructs, which means that we patiently endure suffering and daily choose to do the right thing: The God thing. The Jesus thing. The humble thing.

When you can make this challenging determination and embrace the behavior that the Bible promotes, you will find yourself surrounded by the favor of God! Our goal in dealing with a difficult person, is not to find favor with the person but to find ultimate favor with God. I would rather have favor with God than with people any day of any week of any year of any decade of any century of any millennium!

JUST LIKE JESUS

Jesus is the Perfect Example of how we must behave in all situations in life. Although Jesus was blasphemed, reviled, and cursed by others, He never fought back verbally or physically. He never allowed Himself to be dragged into a war of words. His mouth never sinned! I want to be like Jesus.

Our words will either cause us to fan the flames of the firestorm or to extinguish a fire that has been unfairly set by another person. If we aim our words horizontally toward the instigator of the blaze, it is commensurate to throwing gasoline on the fire, resulting in a burst of searing heat and likely causing harm by the powerful blaze. However, if we only talk to God about the fire, and thereby aim our words vertically toward the Father rather than horizontally toward the fire, the fire will quickly diminish in strength and intensity. As you choose to lift up worship toward the Father, what actually happens is that Heaven sends down a cooling and miraculous shower toward the now-dwindling blaze.

Jesus *"kept entrusting Himself to the Him who judges righteously."* Jesus knew to be true what you and I often ignore: We can trust the Father to have the final word. Jesus committed Himself concerning the unfair words and treatment of others and allowed the Father to do the talking. This phrase, *"kept entrusting Himself,"* is comprised of two Greek words, *para* and *didomi*. *Para* means "alongside, coming along side, choosing to come close to someone," and *didomi* means simply "to give."

When *"para"* and *"didomi"* are paired together, it presents the idea of entrusting something to someone with whom

147

you are very close. It means, in essence, handing something over or yielding something of value to a close friend or an intimate companion. Jesus, in the most difficult and caustic of life situations, yielded His life and the outcome of those situations over to His Father. Jesus didn't have to be in control, because He knew that God, the Judge, would always have the final and righteous say in everything that concerned Him. What an amazing observation this presents! Jesus was the Son of God, and yet He gave His life fully to God the Father and trusted Him with the outcome. Jesus could have whipped His verbal accusers into shape in short order! One word from Jesus, and every person in the angry, cruel mob would have been paralyzed in their devious tracks. But Jesus knew the power of *paradidomi*. Do you?

The decision that Jesus made was not a decision of weakness, but one of supreme and wise strength. When you find yourself in a similar situation and are the victim of raging flames due to the words or choices of an accuser or foe, draw as close as you possibly can to the Father and then yield or trust. Choose not to spew your words horizontally, because that will only add gasoline to the already angry fire. Join Jesus in making a decision of wise strength, and then trust your vertical relationship with your Dad. God wants the very best for you regardless of other people's opinions, accusations, or unkind words. God has favor for you that others are unquestionably unable to offer.

When in a situation where the fire is roaring and fractious people continually add dry, volatile kindling to the increasingly angry fire, two options remain. The first option is to act like a frail human being and become angry, turn sour, and then become defensive. The second and most powerful option is to act like Jesus and choose to be quiet, to submit to God's final say, and to trust Him knowing that He is fully in control.

Your second option includes the submissive yet wise decision of drawing alongside the Father during the hot and decimating time of persecution. It's your choice.

JOB DESCRIPTIONS

> *Therefore humble yourselves under the mighty hand of God, that He may exalt you at the proper time.*
> —1 Peter 5:6

It is very clear, from the words of Peter in this verse, who has been assigned the job of "humbling yourselves" and who has been assigned the job of "exalting". If you do the humbling, I can guarantee you that God will exalt you at the proper time. The problem with this verse is that many of us acquire spiritual dyslexia when reading these particular job descriptions. We are guilty of confusing the job assignments, and we unfortunately take on the job description of God in our own lives. We erroneously think that it is a brilliant idea to exalt self and thereby choose to brag, defend, exaggerate, and pontificate. Satan loves it when he is able to have a human being attempt to participate in self-exalting because that is exactly what the deceiver of the brethren does best. God exalts, my friend, and you have been assigned the very real task of humbling yourself. When you foolishly attempt to exalt yourself, it becomes a painful and dangerous choice.

When dealing with the fires that have been cruelly set by the mouths and choices of others, exalting yourself does not cool the heat of the fire at all. Exalting yourself will only make the fire exponentially hotter and hotter. As the children of God, we are instructed to do the humbling of ourselves and then allow God to do the exalting.

Humbling yourself means to submit yourself in a lowly spirit to the power and the will of God. This is a conscious act of your will and not a knee-jerk reaction to the fires of life. This powerful and godly choice, to humble yourself, does not come naturally to our human flesh. However, joyfully submitting yourself to His care and protection is perhaps the most powerful choice that a believer is able to embrace. The simple truth can be found in the rich answer to this question: *Who can take care of you better? You? Or God?*

God will reverse your past misfortunes, give you triumph over your oppressors, and allow you to participate in Christ's glory when you do the humbling! All of this will happen in God's proper timetable and not in your microwave minute. When we have wisely chosen to humble ourselves, and then when God does not immediately turn things around to our advantage, we often wonder where God is and whether He saw our choice to obey His Word. I can guarantee you for sure and for certain that not one detail of your life has escaped His attention, and He is working behind the scenes of your life to create a masterpiece of His design! God will come through on your behalf when He verifies that there is absolutely no possible opportunity for you to exalt yourself again. That is God's "proper time," and at that time He will rejoice as He moves Heaven and Earth to your personal advantage.

NOT A CARE

And then, after being instructed in what you are expected to do and what God will willingly and extravagantly do in response to your humility, comes one of the most beloved and comforting Scriptures from the entire Bible. Prepare to have your soul comforted with the peace that only the words and heart of Jesus can bring:

> *Casting all your anxiety on Him, because He cares for you.*—1 Peter 5:7

There . . . don't you feel better already?! You can trust Him with your frustrations, your fears, and your worries, because He cares. We serve a God who is concerned about the lives of His beloved children. God cares about the details of your daily existence. He is not oblivious, nor is He ignoring you. He is tenderly involved and concerned about everything that concerns you.

YOUR BEAST OF BURDEN

The word *casting* is a compound word in the Greek built from two words, *epi* and *ripto*. The Greek word *epi* means "on top of something," and the word *ripto* means "to hurl, to throw, to cast, to violently throw, or to fling something with great force."

This word *epiripto* is only used one other time in the entire New Testament:

And they brought him to Jesus: and they cast (epiripto) *their garments upon the colt, and they set Jesus thereon.*—Luke 19:35 KJV

As Jesus entered the city of Jerusalem on the day that we now call Palm Sunday, the people threw their garments and cloaks on the back of the colt before they lifted Jesus up onto the beast of burden. This word *epiripto* implies the bold flinging of excess weight off the shoulders of a traveler and then onto the back of a beast that was designed to carry the baggage.

As common men and women, we have not been designed to carry the burdens of worry, fret, unforgiveness, bitterness, or the cares of life. The load is simply too much for the human body and our central nervous systems to tolerate. If we insist on carrying the massive weights of life, something will break. It is true that for a short season we may be able to carry that which is certainly too heavy for us, but eventually the physical body and the mind will collapse under the unending weight of anxiety and care. The medical world even now admits that some sickness is actually caused or exacerbated by stress, worry, and fear.

The Great Designer of the human body did not design your body with the capacity to carry enormous amounts of negativity, anxiety, and fear. He is calling to you across the ages, and His voice resounds with the sovereign beauty of 1 Peter 5:7.

"Boldly throw every care of your life on Me, because I care about you."

Your shoulders are not muscular enough, nor is your mind massive enough to carry the pain and burdens of Earthbound living. The load will eventually break you, so perhaps you should allow Christ to be your Beast of burden. Take your load and heave it with all of your might on the One who cares, who truly cares, for you. Fling every worry, fear, and stronghold of bitterness in His way, because He was made for the task!

The Greek tells specifically what we are to throw toward Jesus, the One who has been perfectly designed to carry it. The word used in the Greek is *merimna*, which simply and completely means "any anxiety." In its richest definition, *merimna* can mean "any affliction, difficulty, hardship, misfortune, trouble, or complicated circumstances that arise as a result of problems that develop in our lives."

Anything that causes you to worry or to fear, you are supposed to throw in His direction.

Anything that weighs you down, you need to hurl at Him.

Anything that discourages you . . . heave on Him!

Any stress that a fire ushers into your life . . . you are supposed to pitch, with all your human might, toward Him. His back was perfectly designed to carry every single one of your burdens. Nothing is too heavy for His care.

It is ludicrous to imagine what would happen if I were to throw a fifty-pound saddlebag on the back of a rabbit or that of a kitten. Their bones would disintegrate, and their muscles would instantly give way. That is the picture of you and me as we endeavor to hold on to things that we were not made to carry. God, your Father, has the strength and the power to relieve you of everything that causes you to worry. It is what He does best!

HE'S CONCERNED ABOUT YOU

The singular reason He is able to carry all of your cares and anxieties is because He cares. We serve a God who cares. We pray to a God who cares. We worship a God who cares. We throw all of our pain and frustration on a God who cares.

The Greek word *"melei"* is used to describe the One who was perfectly designed to catch and then carry your burdens. The idea that He cares for you is beautifully and expressively summed up in the Greek word , *"melei"*. This word holds a treasure of meanings as it attempts to describe the God who is concerned. *"Melei"* means that He is thoughtful, concerned, interested, caring, aware, and that He notices. This word implies that God, the Catcher of all of our troubles, gives meticulous attention to that which concerns us.

One of the most despicable ploys that the enemy endeavors to employ when a child of God encounters the fiery furnace is that "old liar face" tries to convince God's child that God no longer cares. The devil grins with hateful glee as he declares that God is uninterested in your human pain, that your problems are too stupid, too small, or too inconsequential to heave toward Jesus. Let's clear this up once and for all of eternity: *God cares about you.*

He cares about your problems, big and small. He is interested in the most minute details of your life. He can carry what burdens you. He is concerned about that which has concerned you.

CHAPTER 19

SAFARIS, HALLOWEEN COSTUMES, AND MEOW

RED LEVEL SECURITY ALERT

Be of sober spirit, be on the alert. Your adversary, the devil, prowls around like a roaring lion, seeking someone to devour.—1 Peter 5:8

The words of Peter, written nearly two thousand years ago, are not to be ignored today. It is of vital importance that a believer has a watchful attitude when it comes to the devil. We need to be on high alert to ensure that no enemy aggressor is able to sneak into our territory and gain entrance into any area of our lives. Pay attention, and never be distracted concerning the trickiness of that despotic evil force known as Satan.

When a country engages in warfare, one of the first strategies that is of primary importance is to identify the enemy attacker. Based on the proven identity of the enemy, weapons are then decided upon and strategies are developed. Your enemy is Satan, and he is an enemy of darkness whose only weapon is deceit. You are a soldier of the Light, and the weapons that you have been given in this hand-to-hand combat are the Word of God, worship, prayer, fasting, and giving.

The phrase *"be of sober spirit"* is sometimes translated as *"be watchful."* This is the same Greek word, *"gregoreo,"* that Jesus used when speaking to Peter, James, and John in the Garden of Gethsemane when He asked them to *"watch and pray."* I believe that Jesus is still asking the same thing of His disciples today: *"Watch and pray."* Do not go through the fire and cavalierly ignore the evil intent of enemy forces. "Be watchful and pray" is the best advice ever given to a disciple who is encountering a fire. It is what Jesus chose to do in the most stressful moment of His life, and it is what you should choose to do, as well.

A KITTY CAT

As I study and linger on these verses written by my favorite disciple, Peter, to the early Church and to you and me, I am always astonished by the changes that take place between verses 7 and 8 of this chapter of Scripture.

Casting all your anxiety on Him, because He cares for you.

Be of sober spirit, be on the alert. Your adversary, the devil, prowls around like a roaring lion, seeking someone to devour.

What a profound juxtaposition between these two paramount verses. The message of Peter began with great compassion and with the sincere communication of God's absolute care for His children. Then, immediately, Peter takes a gargantuan plunge into spiritual warfare against the enemy of all enemies! How did Peter leap from eternal loving-kindness to that dastardly roaring kitty cat who only portends to be a vicious lion?

God's care and love are all the preparation that you need in order to victoriously encounter that declawed, defanged feline that is atrociously stalking God's children. Peter reminds the reader that the devil is not a roaring lion, but that he merely pretends to be one. The devil is old Snaggletooth himself, with a hacking cough that he believes to be a biting roar. All this enemy has is sound with no true power or authority. He is all bark and no bite. He is a sickly, disguised character dressed up in last year's Halloween costume.

One way in which the devil is indeed similar to real-life lions is that lions are known for attacking sick, young, or straggling prey. This, too, is the identical scheme of the enemy. He goes after believers who are young in their faith, who are sick in body, soul, or mind, or those who are alone. The devil chooses his victims carefully, and he only goes after those who are not alert or those who are detached from the family.

The roar of a ravenous lion is absolutely deafening! The thunder that begins in the belly of a lion and then explodes out of his mouth echoes across the prairies of his habitat. Always remind yourself that the roar of the enemy may be cacophonous and crashing, but it holds absolutely no authority or threat.

What the devil does want to do is eat you for lunch. His intent is to terrify you with his roar and then destroy your faith, rob you of your joy, and turn you into a cowardly kitten confined to a corner for the rest of your life. Lions are known for stalking their prey, for observing their habits, and for closely following them with watchful focus. The devil has been watching you for a lifetime and has become well-acquainted with your likes and dislikes, with your preferences, and with your weaknesses. That is why you need to be watchful every minute of every day!

The strategy of a lion in attacking prey is called "cooperative hunting." A pride of female lions or a cooperative of male lions will surround their prey, and then only one of the lions will let off a thunderous and earsplitting roar. While the prey runs in the opposite direction of the roar, it will run straight into the mouth of another lion. It is the fear of the roar that literally kills the unsuspecting prey. It is fear that causes the prey to run in the wrong direction. It is fear that will cause you to be a victim of the enemy, as well.

YOU'RE GOING ON A LION HUNT

When you join a safari or a lion hunt, part of the training and preparation includes what to do in case of a lion attack. These same safari safety principles may aid the children of God when encountering a catlike enemy who falsely believes himself to be a lion. These three principles certainly present a wise and victorious strategy for anyone who comes in contact with the wildcat of the kingdom of darkness.

1 – Never try to flee. Running away means certain death, and a lion is able to run much faster than a human being. When you encounter the devil, the one who should be doing the fleeing is actually the creature who is impersonating the lion. Your instructions for this safari known as "life" are to submit to God and resist the enemy. That is the tactic that the Bible offers when dealing with the fake feline.

Submit therefore to God. Resist the devil and he will flee from you.—James 4:7

2 – Be very brave. Look the lion straight in the eye. Often a lion will back down and walk away when he or she meets a more courageous species. Lions generally don't know how to deal with those who stand up to them and stare them down.

3 – However, if the first two strategies don't work for you, be prepared for an attack. Raise your spear in the air so that when the lion rushes toward you, the attacking creature will land directly on your spear.

Do you have an available spear? Is your spear sharpened and ready to kill an encroaching and aggressive lion? Your spear is the sword of the Spirit, which is the Word of God!

And take the helmet of salvation, and the sword of the Spirit, which is the word of God.—Ephesians 6:17

Remind yourself daily that Satan is not actually a roaring lion, but he merely has on a ridiculous and cheap Halloween costume. Underneath that preposterous getup, he is in reality a weak, whining, pip-squeak of a character with an overrated voice box.

Not only does the courageous Peter portray Satan as a catlike creature creeping around, but his description also identifies him as an adversary.

This word *adversary* is better defined as a prosecutor in a court of law who is known for bringing innocent victims to court, savagely arguing against them, bringing up untruths, and then sending the innocent persons to prison. This is an accurate picture of the schemes of the devil, who strikes like a cruel and manipulative lawyer, uses lies and half truths against the children of God, and then puts the victims in lifetime sentences of chains. John, in the Book of the Revelation, refers to Satan as "the accuser of the brethren."

RESIST!

But resist him, firm in your faith, knowing that the same experiences of suffering are being accomplished by your brethren who are in the world.—1 Peter 5:9

The advice of Peter and the Holy Spirit that resounds through the ages to your life can be uttered in one single word: *"Resist!"* The only way that you are able to resist the enemy is by being firm in your faith. Faith is the shield that fights off the fiery darts of the enemy, and it provides the strong resistance that is needed when he is trying to eat you for his tasty lunch. Your emotions are not strong enough to enable you to resist this insidious creature who insists on

159

tormenting the people of God. Powerful resistance always entails declaring the Word of God over the situations that the enemy has stirred up and set on fire.

Faith comes from hearing, and hearing by the word of Christ.—Romans 10:17

The Word of God gives powerful authority over and resistance to the scrawny, emaciated, catlike creature who tries to intimidate us with his roar. The Word of God is the spear that the devil will fall on time after time after time.

Submit therefore to God. Resist the devil and he will flee from you. Draw near to God and He will draw near to you.—James 4:7–8

And finally, when in hand-to-hand combat with this pauper of no means who falsely believes that he is the king of the jungle, the advice of James is to *"draw near to God."* Draw near to the God who cares for you. Draw near to the God who is the Holder of all eternal strength and power. Draw near to the God who defeated the enemy at the Cross of Calvary. Draw near to God.

Jesus kept entrusting himself to the One who judges righteously; the advice of James is in complete agreement with the actions and the example of Jesus. Jesus continually drew himself alongside His Father because He knew that that decision was a power strategy for enemy attacks. Jesus knew, for sure and for certain, that the fires of life were no match for the God of Heaven. You might want to consider doing what Jesus did during His stay on Earth: *Stay close to the General!*

NEVER ALONE

Knowing that the same experiences of suffering are

being accomplished by your brethren who are in the world."—1 Peter 5:9

You are not the only Christian on the enemy's radar screen, so do not get prideful and believe that this is all about you. The devil has never taken kindly to men and women of faith, and what he is actually attacking is faith in its purest form. The devil doesn't actually care about you and your life, because what he wants to devour is your faith so that you are unable to walk in the power and authority that you were created to walk in. The devil wants to steal your joy, which is what enables you to be the strongest version of yourself. The devil wants to devour your peace, so that you will be unable to trust the Lord. The devil wants to abscond with your wisdom, so that you will act foolishly. To the enemy, you are simply an unknown, unnamed ends to a means. The devil's chief goal in your life is to diminish the glory of God that is inside of you.

In every century, during every epoch, the enemy has endeavored to intimidate the people of God. Ask Daniel what those hungry lions sounded like! Ask David about the colossal size of Goliath! Ask Shadrach, Meshach, and Abednego about the searing temperatures of the fiery furnace! Ask Moses about the loneliness in the wilderness! Ask Jonah what the inside of a fish smells like! Ask Paul about the turbulence that occurred just before a violent shipwreck!

And while you are at it . . . ask Corrie ten Boom about the cruelty in a concentration camp. Ask John and Betty Stam what it felt like to be beheaded in China. Ask Richard Wurmbrand what it was like to be tortured for Christ. Ask Jim Elliot what it felt like to be on the other end of a sword from an Auca Indian.

Every hero and heroine of the faith who has met the

enemy in the back alley of torturous circumstances will respond to our interrogation with determined truth and with power: *"God was with me! He never left me alone! His joy surrounded me like a shield, and I found His presence to be more than enough!"*

AFTER THE ATTACK

After you have suffered for a little while, the God of all grace, who called you to His eternal glory in Christ, will Himself perfect, confirm, strengthen and establish you. To Him be dominion forever and ever. Amen.—1 Peter 5:10–11

It is guaranteed, according to the Word of God, that you will come out of an attack by the enemy better than before you encountered the attack! In the natural, this makes absolutely no sense. After an attack in battle, soldiers usually come out with wounds, with shrapnel in their bodies, and with post-traumatic stress disorder. However, as soldiers in the army of Christ, after a battle with the enemy, we come out with a divine and holy makeover! We are miraculously perfected, confirmed, strengthened, and established.

When a soldier of Christ encounters enemy fire and chooses to fight with faith and with worship, God is able to perfect this valiant soldier. God restores whatever the enemy has taken and then mends what sin has broken. God gloriously equips this perfected soldier with the strength to get back into action!

Then, the greatest General in all of recorded history is able to confirm the direction of His fabulous fighting forces. He turns them resolutely in His chosen direction and helps them to set their minds on things that are above, not things that are on the Earth. Rather than focusing on enemy terrain, a soldier in God's army focuses on the glory that is to come!

After encountering the enemy and coming through the battle with faith and with worship, God then takes His courageous soldier and strengthens him or gives him back his vigor. It is possible, through Christ, to be more vigorous and renewed after the fire than before the fire. There can be a new resolve in the soldier's soul and an anticipation of all that is yet ahead!

And finally, God takes a war-weary soldier who has declared the Word of God with his or her hands raised in the air, and God is able to establish this soldier in a place with a solid and eternal foundation. The life that God now offers to someone with battle experience is so solid and so extraordinary that it will endure the test of time and eternity.

The trials and fires of life, whether set by circumstances or by people, will be used by God for extreme benefit and for blessing. God is able to take the life that has encountered trials, fires, and battles, and turn it into a life of pure-gold blessing and substance!

CHAPTER 20
HONORABLE FIRES

I HAVE NEVER APPRECIATED the Book of Job in the Bible. I tend to be a turtle when it comes to discussing other people's pain, and I often cowardly withdraw from difficult and distressing conversations. I am much more like Pollyanna in my approach to life, and I find great delight in playing the glad game. Studying the Book of Job is out of character for my naïve, "let's ignore the pain" life philosophy that I have erroneously embraced!

The Book of Job is nestled in the first part of the Old Testament, just before the powerful Book of Psalms. Somehow I have always thought that the positioning of Job in the Bible was appropriate. The discomfort of the Book of Job needs the comfort of Psalms to follow its pain, just like I need goodness and mercy to follow me all the days of my life!

It's not that I am afraid of the Book of Job . . . I just have absolutely no desire to relate to Job and his tragic life. Perhaps I secretly wonder if all of the horrible things that happened to Job are contagious across the sands of time. If that is true, I certainly don't want to get anywhere close to Job's calamitous germs! If you were honest, you might admit that you feel exactly the same way about this ancient man and his cataclysmic circumstances.

I suppose at the heart of my aversion to the Book of Job is that I don't actually want to know why this honorable man of God was targeted by the enemy. I don't want to know why bad things happen to good people, but I just want to singularly focus on the fact that God is good, all the time. There is no bad in God. He is enthusiastically, perpetually, and radically good! Somehow I feel safe and secure in reminding myself of the irrefutable fact that God's goodness is all that I need to get through the bad days of my life.

However, the truth remains that there was a man by the name of Job, and that the Holy Spirit, who is an Expert at everything, thought that Job's story was important enough to place it in the Bible. Job undoubtedly lived, and the Bible evaluates his life as vital enough to the complete message of God to tell through the sacred pages of my very favorite Book. Job legitimately suffered, even though he was a good man. More precisely, Job was a great man. Job was perhaps one of the greatest to have ever lived in any historical epoch. And yet, this man of righteousness and valor was no stranger to the extreme heat of the fires of life.

As much as I hate to admit it, the truth is this: In order to obtain a complete, biblical view and a correct theology of how the difficult experiences in life are able to refine us, we must study this book and the life of this man by the name of Job. Let's travel through time and take a long and focused look at the life of a man who really lived, who suffered acute and relentless pain, and who chose to continue to worship in spite of horrific and hot circumstances. There is something in the life of Job for all of us.

A MAN NAMED JOB

There was a man in the land of Uz whose name was Job; and that man was blameless, upright, fearing God and turning away from evil. Seven sons and three daughters were born to him. His possessions also were 7,000 sheep, 3,000 camels, 500 yoke of oxen, 500 female donkeys, and very many servants; and that man was the greatest of all the men of the east.—Job 1:1–3

The Bible describes Job as a man among men who was truly good all the way through. Often, when I read the description of Job in the Bible, I wonder how the Holy Spirit would describe my own life. I am compelled and challenged by the description of Job in the Bible to live in a way that honors God and honors others.

Job was blameless, upright, fearing God, and turning away from evil; the Bible describes this man among men as "the greatest of all the men of the east." Job quite simply did everything well in the sight of God. He had his priorities straight, and if ever temptation came his way, he was able to choose the right and shun the wrong.

The Bible describes this man Job with one singular term that definitively evokes admiration and high respect on his behalf: *blameless*. The word *blameless* is used sparingly in the Word of God, due to the fact that not many human beings have achieved the honor of being described by this exemplary term.

If anyone can be described as "*blameless*," God certainly deserves that sterling and honorable description. The Bible, therefore, understandably and understatedly describes God as "*blameless*":

> *"As for God, His way is blameless; the word of the Lord is tested; He is a shield to all who take refuge in Him."*—2 Samuel 22:31

Jesus, God's own Son, is also described by using this perfect term *blameless*. This is what the Bible says concerning the Lamb of God, God's Son, who was our sacrifice:

> *Knowing that you were not redeemed with perishable things like silver or gold from your futile way of life inherited from your forefathers, but with precious blood, as of a lamb unblemished and spotless, the blood of Christ.*—1 Peter 1:18–19

Noah is another Old Testament figure who, in addition

to Job, is described as being "*blameless*" in the eyes of God:

> *These are the records of the generations of Noah. Noah was a righteous man, blameless in his time; Noah walked with God.*—Genesis 6:9

Noah and Job made the list! They are the top two men of the Old Testament who are described with the exact same adjective as God the Father and as Jesus, His Son. Other people in the Bible are encouraged to be blameless or are described as being "blameless" in a singular situation in life. However, when *blameless* is used as a descriptive adjective in the Old Testament to describe a person's complete lifestyle, it is only God the Father, Jesus the Son, Noah, and Job who are described in such a way.

However, there is one more addition to this "*blameless*" list in the Bible, which can be found in the New Testament. There is one other group of people whom the Holy Spirit has determined is worthy of this pure and holy adjective, "blameless":

> *Blessed be the God and Father of our Lord Jesus Christ, who has blessed us with every spiritual blessing in the heavenly places in Christ, just as He chose us in Him before the foundation of the world, that we would be holy and blameless before Him.*—Ephesians 1:3–4

Because you have Jesus, you are also the beneficiary of His blameless nature! Because Jesus died on the Cross for your sins and because you have received Him into your heart, you stand blameless before the throne of God for all of eternity. You have become like Him, not because of your actions, but because of His action. His blood has covered all of your sin for time and eternity, and now Heaven describes your life as being "blameless"! What a high honor and privilege! You are now described as having the same characteristic as God because of His Son, Jesus Christ!

Noah, God, Jesus, Job, *and you* have this stellar adjective in common: The Bible considers you *"blameless"*!

BLAMELESS, BUT ATTACKED

The blameless Job was not immune to the attack of the enemy. Even blameless people like Jesus and Job encounter the enemy and are targets of his unfair schemes. Sin is not a prerequisite to suffering, so when you observe someone who is going through enemy fire, do not automatically presume that they have done something to deserve it. The truth is, perhaps it is their blameless life that has set them in the crossfire of the enemy's attacks.

> *His sons used to go and hold a feast in the house of each one on his day, and they would send and invite their three sisters to eat and drink with them. When the days of feasting had completed their cycle, Job would send and consecrate them, rising up early in the morning and offering burnt offerings according to the number of them all; for Job said, "Perhaps my sons have sinned and cursed God in their hearts." Thus Job did continually.*—Job 1:4–5

The Book of Job was written during the days of the Patriarchs, which includes Abraham, Isaac, and Jacob. During this period of history, the father of the family was the family's religious leader. In these verses, Job was acting as the priest of his family and offered sacrifices to ask for forgiveness of behalf of his sons. Before Christ and Calvary, the only way to access God was through a blood sacrifice. The blameless Job wanted to make sure that all of his children were able to go to Heaven when they died, so he offered blood sacrifices on their behalf.

> *Now there was a day when the sons of God came to*

present themselves before the Lord, and Satan also came
among them. The Lord said to Satan, "From where
do you come?" Then Satan answered the Lord and
said, "From roaming about on the earth and walking
around on it."—Job 1:6–7

Satan had been roaming around on Planet Earth for the
express purpose of seeking someone to devour. This word
roaming is from the Hebrew word *shuwt*, and it literally means
"inspecting your land." Satan had been checking out the real
estate of God and of His people. The New Testament also uses a
word from the Greek that describes Satan as "roaming," as well.

Be of sober spirit, be on the alert. Your adversary,
the devil, prowls around like a roaring lion, seeking
someone to devour.—1 Peter 5:8

The word *roams* from this verse in 1 Peter 5:8 is best
translated as "to make due use of an opportunity." The
blameless you and the blameless Job fight the same enemy,
and his strategy has not changed in the thousands of years
since Job lived on Earth. The enemy still engages himself in
"roaming." He is inspecting your land and will make due use
of every opportunity that comes his rotten little way.

THINGS HAVE CHANGED FOR THE ENEMY

In the Old Testament, Satan possessed a greater presence
and power than he does today for the people of God who
have been bought with the blood of the Lamb. After Calvary,
because of the work and ultimate victory of Jesus, the works of
Satan have been destroyed, so he no longer has the power to
enact a Job-like attack on your life. Satan is still roaming . . .
he is just hanging out like a hoodlum on a street corner in the
dark of night, but he no longer holds any power at all. Jesus
has given all of His power to you, the blameless!

The Son of God appeared for this purpose, to destroy the works of the devil.—1 John 3:8

Jesus came to Earth for this powerful purpose: to destroy the works of the one who roams! Satan no longer has the power that he had in the Book of Job, because Calvary changed everything!

Therefore when Jesus had received the sour wine, He said, "It is finished!" And He bowed His head and gave up His spirit.—John 19:30

When Jesus cried out, *"It is finished!"* on the Cross of Calvary, it was because He had completed what He had come to Earth to accomplish. His job and His purpose were complete. He had destroyed the works of the devil for time and for all of eternity. Calvary ripped the power out of Satan's bag of tricks and only left him with deceit. Satan is still hanging around like a juvenile delinquent on the perimeter of your life. He loiters menacingly in the back alleys looking for an opportunity to deceive you out of your birthright, but his power has been utterly and thoroughly destroyed. As the light of the world at your moment in history, you have been called and empowered to shine the light of Christ that exists in you into Satan's darkness and onto the back allies in which he is loitering.

In addition to being the light of the world, you also have the Word of God to use in the skirmishes with the enemy that he tries to incite:

The Lord said to Satan, "Have you considered My servant Job? For there is no one like him on the earth, a blameless and upright man, fearing God and turning away from evil." Then Satan answered the Lord, "Does Job fear God for nothing? Have You not made a hedge about him and his house and all that he has, on every *side? You have blessed the work of his hands, and his possessions have increased in the land. But put forth Your hand now and touch all that he has; he will surely curse You to Your face." Then the Lord said to Satan, "Behold, all that he has is in your power, only do not put forth your hand on him." So Satan departed from the presence of the Lord.—*Job 1:8–12

Satan was up to his dastardly ways and had been roaming and looking for someone whom he could devour. God knew Job's character and Job's heart. God was intimately acquainted with Job and all of his ways. God knew that no matter what Satan attempted to do to Job, Job would still be found blameless. Satan falsely believed that Job only trusted God because God had protected and blessed Job. God knew that Job would trust Him regardless of the attacks or the schemes of the enemy.

This battle, between Satan and Job, would be one for the ages.

AN ATTACK THAT ECHOES STILL

On one singular day, Job lost everything. He lost his oxen, donkeys, sheep, camels, and servants. But the most horrific blow of all was that on that terrible day, a tornadic wind blew in, and all ten of his beloved children were killed in an instant.

The response of a man or a woman to an undeserved and searing fire in life is perhaps the most accurate thermometer of all. How you respond when dealing with abhorrent and dreadful events reveals your trust for God and the depth of revelation of His character and goodness in your life.

No one, least of all you or me, would blame Job for questioning God and spending years in deep grief and self-pity. If any person has ever deserved to question God, it is

Job. If any person has ever deserved to feel sorry for himself, it is Job. If any person has ever been justified in wallowing in human pain and emotion, it is Job. However, Job chose to exhibit none of those human justifications. Job, the blameless man who was the greatest man alive, chose something much different, indeed.

BLAMELESS PEOPLE DON'T BLAME

Then Job arose and tore his robe and shaved his head, and he fell to the ground and worshiped. He said, "Naked I came from my mother's womb, and naked I shall return there. The Lord gave and the Lord has taken away. Blessed be the name of the Lord." Through all this Job did not sin nor did he blame God.—Job 1:20–22

Are you, like me, encased in guilt and regret as you read the heartfelt and pure words of this man named Job? His entire family had been wiped out in one day, and yet he chose to worship the Lord at the very worst moment of his life. Oh, that this was my testimony! Oh, that I would fall on my face and worship the Lord instantly when suffering from the pain and the blistering of fourth-degree burns!

This verse implies that blaming God would be a sin, because it says, *"Through all this Job did not sin nor did he blame God."* The implication is that if Job had chosen to blame God for his horrific life circumstances, it would have been a sin. From the life of this blameless man, Job, we learn that it is possible to grieve without blaming God. It is apparent from this man's blameless life that it is possible to encounter a broken heart without blaming God. It is also possible to suffer from third- and fourth-degree burns without blaming God. Grief is an allowable human emotion, and while we grieve, God gathers us in His loving and compassionate arms and tenderly breathes on us. His breath is what restores our souls during days of horrific pain.

Job was not the only man who worshiped during days of intense human pain; David, also, the man after God's own heart, chose to worship God on the day of his son's death:

> *But when David saw that his servants were whispering together, David perceived that the child was dead; so David said to his servants, "Is the child dead?" And they said, "He is dead." So David arose from the ground, washed, anointed himself, and changed his clothes; and he came into the house of the Lord and worshiped.*—2 Samuel 12: 19–20

David worshiped while he grieved the loss of his little boy; Job worshiped while he grieved the loss of his entire family. The enemy desires to place you in a position where you will be tempted to blame God, but blameless people inevitably choose to worship God! If there is no blame in your heart, it will be impossible to blame God on the worst day of your life. It is impossible for blameless men and blameless women to blame God; their only and genuine response to heartbreak and to the fires of life is to worship God while on their faces. A blameless person, and that is what you are according to the Word of God, has no blame inside his or her heart when life crashes down around them. The song of their hearts overcomes the temptation to blame, and the unquenchable melody of worship rises above the sorrow of life.

This is an issue of pure-gold significance in the life of a believer: What will you do during days of intense grief and emotional pain? Worship transcends understanding, because you do not need to "understand" your circumstances in order to worship God. Trust transcends understanding, because you do not need to "understand" your circumstances in order to trust the God who is always good. Peace surpasses understanding, because you do not need to "understand" circumstances in order to be the recipient of God's peace.

During the grief process, you are allowed to cry, but if all you are doing is weeping, you are only doing half the job! You can cry . . . but worship, as well. You can weep . . . but trust, as well! You can wail . . . but receive His peace in the process.

HOW DO YOU SPELL "RELIEF"?

Satan continued his perusal of the territory of Job and the terrain of Job's life, and then asked for an appointment with God. The Lord pointed out to Satan that even though Satan had endeavored to incite Job against God and had also tried to ruin him without cause, Job held fast to his integrity. The Lord told Satan concerning Job:

> *"There is no one like him on the earth, a blameless and upright man fearing God and turning away from evil."*—Job 2:3

The enemy was not content with the portion of Job's life that he had been given, and he thus asked for Job's skin, as well. Satan falsely believed that if he could put Job in tormenting and physical pain, Job would curse God to His face. God told Satan that He would allow him to cause physical pain to Job's life, but that God would not allow the enemy to kill Job.

> *Then Satan went out from the presence of the Lord and smote Job with sore boils from the sole of his foot to the crown of his head.*—Job 2:7

If losing all of his oxen, donkeys, sheep, camels, servants, and children in one twenty-four-hour period wasn't enough for one man, then the vicious and despicable Satan afflicted the blameless Job with ugly, crusty, painful boils over his entire body. There was not a millimeter on Job's blameless body that was not inflicted with the torture of cruel, miserable boils.

> *And he took a potsherd to scrape himself while he was sitting among the ashes. Then his wife said to him, "Do you still hold fast your integrity? Curse God and die!" But he said to her, "You speak as one of the foolish women speaks. Shall we indeed accept good from God and not accept adversity?" In all this Job did not sin with his lips.*—Job 2:8–10

Job did not sin with his lips; he refused, with every ounce of life in him, to blame the Lord, whom he knew to be a God of goodness and of blessing. Satan's despotic plan is to place humanity in a situation in life where they are tempted to sin with their lips; Satan wants God's beloved children to blame God, when in reality, the devil is the evil one who deserves all of the blame for every painful situation in life. Satan wants you to doubt God when your life is falling apart, but God wants you to trust Him. God wants you to honor Him and worship Him. Whose wishes will you adhere to? Whose heart will you please?

Into the story of Job enter three of his closest friends, by the names of Eliphaz, Bildad, and Zophar. These three might as well have been named "Curly," "Larry," and "Moe," because of their laughable, Stooge-like responses. This trio of chumps was sadly unable to offer comfort and wisdom to their godly and blameless friend. These three clowns were quiet for seven days and for seven nights as they realized how deep was the pain of the greatest man on the face of the Earth, Job. These men should have kept their mouths firmly closed rather than choosing to say what is recorded in Scripture. However, because Job's comforters actually had the audacity to blame the blameless Job for his suffering, they smugly informed him that he needed to repent.

God's opinion of Job was that he was blameless; the opinion of Eliphaz, Bildad, and Zophar was that Job had sinned and so he somehow, in some twisted way, deserved his suffering. The three foolish friends were no comfort at all. Instead they added to the unremitting and horrific pain that had taken up residence in Job's broken heart.

FORGIVE THEM ANYWAY

When five of my babies died in my womb at between twelve and twenty weeks in my pregnancies, I was overwhelmed by women who had good intentions but who also possessed the same lack of compassion that Job's comforters possessed. There were women who told me it was my fault that the babies were dying, and there were women who told that it wasn't God's will for me to have any more children. There were women who said that I ate too much, and some women said I ate too little. Some women said that I was too active, while others said that I wasn't active enough. Job's comforters were not peculiar only to Job and to his tragedy. Anyone who has ever walked through any type of human pain knows the challenge of being emotionally stomped upon by stooges who falsely believe they are loyal friends.

During my days of great grief and emotional pain, while my arms were empty and my heart was raw, I determined just to go ahead and forgive anyone for anything painful that they might say to me concerning my sorrow. I decided not to receive any judgmental declarations over my life, but to whisper a heartfelt prayer of forgiveness as my Eliphazes, Bildads, and Zophars stomped all over my raw heart and then walked away.

When going through the fires of life, it is of vital importance to your future emotional and spiritual health that you make the choice to forgive foolish people for all of the wrong and hurtful words that they may speak quickly and decisively. Decide ahead of time that you are an unoffendable Christian and that the ugly and foolish words spoken to you on the worst day of your life will hold no power over your life.

People are not perfect! Only God is perfect, so go to Him with your questions and with your grief. He is able to comfort you in a way that no other is able to. Food cannot comfort you like God can; shopping cannot comfort you like Jesus can. Do not expect people to be to you what only God can be to you. He is the God of all comfort, so wrap yourself in His arms of love when you are covered with the boils of human pain and tragedy.

When others blame you and blame God, make a willful decision to lift up the name of Jesus and to worship the power of the eternal God.

BACK TO THE STOOGES

Zophar then gave full vent to a long and harsh diatribe, explaining from his perspective why this horrific calamity was all Job's fault. Bildad chimed in with the astute foolishness that because God only rewards the good, if Job had been a good man, then he would not be experiencing this tragic pain. Zophar and Bildad certainly were experts at kicking a man when he was down!

This is how the blameless Job responded to his stooges:

"With Him are wisdom and might; to Him belong counsel and understanding."—Job 12:13

Job was reminding the three most foolish men who ever lived that no one in all of recorded history has ever had a better idea than God! Job was declaring that although he was unable to understand the circumstances of his life, he fully trusted the wisdom of God. Job knew, as was revealed in his speech and in his heart, that God had the power and the wisdom to orchestrate and have the resounding and final words in Job's singular and ordinary life.

When in Job-like conditions, it is important to remember that as humans, we are unable to comprehend the heart and the ways of God. That is why it is imperative that your very first thought while in the fire must be *God is good.*

Declare it: *"God is good."*

Memorize it: *"God is always good."*

Sing it: *"Lord, You are good all the time."*

Think it: *"I know that I know that I know that God is good."*

Quote it: *"God is good and He brings only good into my life."*

Meditate on it: *"God is good . . . there is no bad in Him."*

Repeat it: *"God is so good . . . His goodness is unable to be measured!"*

Pray it: *"God, thank You that Your goodness is aimed at my life today!"*

God is good . . . He is infinitely, enthusiastically, and perpetually good. Although we are unable to understand the ways of God, what we can comprehend in our limited human ability is that we serve a God who is good. Always. All the time.

JOB AND HIS SENSE OF HUMOR

"With Him are strength and sound wisdom, the misled and the misleader belong to Him."—Job 12:16

Job was telling this ridiculous triumvirate of foolish men

179

exactly what they were: They were misleaders of the worst
kind! Job might have had a twinkle in his eye in spite of
his boils when he reminded the stooges that although their
thinking was askew, all three of them still belonged to God.
Job, in his humorous remark, was referring to himself as the
"misled." He was letting this trio of off-key theologians know
that they were the misleaders and that he was the misled. Job
was trying, in spite of his human pain, to point their hearts
and minds back to the God who always gives strength and
sound wisdom.

"Though He slay me, I will hope in Him."—Job 13:15

And with these infamous words, Job declared across the
ages the encouragement that would ricochet through every
epoch, every century, every year, and every suffering soul.
Job was pronouncing as a theological reminder to you and to
me, "No matter what happens in my life, I will yet trust in
my God!" This is the powerful statement that all blameless
people choose to make in the face of tragedy, foolish friends,
and unanswered questions.

Have you made that determination yet? Have you decided
that regardless of the intensity of the fire and the searing
temperatures of the flame, you will place all of your hope in
God alone? It is the highest wisdom to boldly establish that
determination of trust during the tranquil and sweet days of
life, so that when the fire comes you have the strength to
default to hope. Hope, for the believer, is our default setting.
Pain and the fires of life are unavoidable, but the choice of
hope remains certain and victorious.

But the story of Job doesn't end here . . . read on, my
friend, read on.

CHAPTER 21
AS FOR ME!

"As for me, I know that my Redeemer lives, and at the last He will take His stand on the earth. Even after my skin is destroyed, yet from my flesh I shall see God; whom I myself shall behold, and whom my eyes will see and not another."—Job 19:25–27

Job began his immortal soliloquy with the powerful pronouncement, *"As for me . . ."* The stooges could foolishly make their own personal theological choices, but Job had resolved that he would live for the One who had conceived of his life before the oceans were given their boundaries. Job would trust the One who lived eternally because He was the only One who deserved no blame. Job would find hope knowing that he would certainly see God one day. Job had placed his focus, in this life and in the next, on the God who had redeemed his life.

Each one of us must individually predispose how to behave in the middle of torturous pain and what to believe in the middle of the roaring fire. The words that you speak while in a trial reveal your intimacy with God and your knowledge of who He is. The words that you choose to speak while dealing with the scorching heat of circumstantial fires will answer this singular life question: *Is the fire for God within you greater than the fire around you?*

As for me . . . God is good and I will declare it!

As for me . . . I will declare His goodness over all my dashed dreams and shattered heart.

As for me . . . I will worship Him while others wail and whine!

As for me . . . I will always bless Him and never blame Him!

As for me!

While Job's foolish trio of friends pontificated, falsified, and blamed, Job determined that his mouth would glorify God. Job informed this famous trio of clowns that they could choose to say whatever they wanted to say, but . . . *as for me . . .* my Redeemer lives!

PERPETUAL WORSHIP

To grant those who mourn in Zion, giving them a garland instead of ashes, the oil of gladness instead of mourning, the mantle of praise instead of a spirit of fainting. So they will be called oaks of righteousness, the planting of the Lord, that He may be glorified.—Isaiah 61:3

"Zion," when referenced in the Old Testament, was the high place of worship where the priests were known to have lived. As New Testament priests, we are called to live in a perpetual state of praise and worship. If a believer is able to turn a place of mourning into a place of worship, the benefits will be three extraordinary, too-good-to-be-true gifts from God the Father. For those who choose to worship rather than whine and wail, God gives:

1 – A garland, or a crown, that signifies royalty.

2 – The oil of gladness, which means a bounty of joy! This oil of gladness was used at banquets or celebrations as a symbol of inexpressible joy.

3 – The mantle of praise, which was the garment of the choir. God will recognize true worshipers and give them opportunities to sing forth the attributes of God as they travel through life.

However, if a person chooses to blame or wail rather

than worship, the benefits become paralyzing and burdensome deficits:

1 – Ashes, or the identification as one who is in constant mourning.

2 – The mourner's cry, or a sound of wailing that is loud and shrill rather than a song.

3 – A weakened condition of living, which is a spirit of fainting. This signifies something that is failing, a wick that is extinguishing, or eyes that are going blind.

Which list do you prefer? Which list will identify you as you travel through life in the fire? You will be the recipient of whichever list you choose. God desires that your life would be the demonstrative example of a priest who worships rather than wails and therefore lives a life of extravagant blessing. God wants to bestow upon your life the first list of advantages, and He desires that your place of pain would become a rich and glorious place of praise. If you can open your mouth in worship, God will turn the waste places and the wilderness of your life into a well-watered and flourishing garden. If you will bless God rather than blame Him, your fire has the potential to become the very finest hour of your life.

WHAT WILL YOU CHOOSE?

One of the most valuable and riveting choices one will ever make is *"Will I worship in the fire?"* The truth is that what you choose while in the fire has a lifetime of impact. The determination to worship when everything in your life is being incinerated has more impact than does your salary, your education level, your street address, or your circle of friends. You will be the recipient of what you have chosen.

Job chose worship!

David chose worship!

Paul and Silas chose worship!

Hannah chose worship!

Abraham chose worship!

You are not alone as you stand at the crossroads of "worship" and "blame," but you stand at that riveting place with the saints of the ages. One of the lies of the despicable enemy is to get you to believe that you stand at that strategic place alone. Satan tries to convince you, as you stare at the signs that say BLAME and WORSHIP, that you stand there unattended and unaccompanied. Satan has lied to every man and every woman of God while in the furnace of great affliction, "You are alone. Pitifully alone." The enemy endeavors to deceive you into believing that no one has ever experienced your pain, and that no one else, on the face of the entire planet, is capable of understanding your personal and unique fire.

You are not alone, my friend! Generations of believers who came before you had to make this same life-altering choice of whether to worship God or to blame God. Thousands of believers today stand at that same crossroads and are willing to join their hands and their voices with yours in the determination to worship—to simply and powerfully worship.

However, the imperative remains: Even if none will sing with you . . . sing anyway! If no one else is worshiping God . . . worship alone! If everyone else has decided to blame God . . . be the singular voice of your generation who has defiantly chosen to bless the Lord with every cell of your existence!

DECLARATION REVEALS HEART

"But He knows the way I take; when He has tried me, I shall come forth as gold."—Job 23:10

The declaration of Job's lips reveals the purity of Job's heart. In the midst of intense, personal pain, Job knew that he was also in the middle of the careful process of God. Job knew that as long as he released the dross and kept his human eyes on his eternal and good Father, gold would be the result! Job understood what you and I often ignore: that the purpose of the fire is coming forth as gold. Job was determined to come forth as gold, thus bearing the reflection of his Maker in its sheen.

Finally, when Job's three confused friends had nothing else to say in the presence of the greatest man who ever lived, God spoke up! When the three foolish men took a breath due to the fact that they had run out of hot air, God began to give His opinion on the matter.

One of the most pivotal points in anyone's fire is when one is able to determine who is speaking on behalf of God and who is speaking on behalf of self and foolishness. It is vital to discern God's voice in the fire, because others will claim to speak on behalf of God. Do not listen to the foolishness and misleading words of those who have chosen to blame God and to blame people. Wait in the place of worship until God speaks His heart in the middle of the blaze of your fire.

Often, this is a difficult determination to discern. Perhaps a wise litmus test is that fools will minimize the power of God and will limit His power. Those who have stood at the crossroads of WORSHIP and BLAME and have chosen to follow the path marked WORSHIP will always point toward the power and the goodness of God. The choice to stay on the path marked WORSHIP will always take a weary traveler and firefighter to a place called Hope.

GROW UP!

Then the Lord answered Job out of the whirlwind and said, "Who is this that darkens counsel by words without knowledge?"—Job 38:1–2

When the Lord inserted His eternal and wise opinion, the first words out of His holy mouth were, *"Who in the world are these ranting, foolish men who don't even know what they are talking about?"* God was in total agreement with the blameless Job concerning the heart condition of these three impotent friends. And then, God inserted His humor into their reality:

"Now gird up your loins like a man, and I will ask you, and you instruct Me!"—Job 38:3

Can you bear with me for a minute for a little break from the intensity of Job's life and see the humor of God's statement? God, the Creator of the universe and the Giver of life, was telling Job and the three buffoons to "man up"! He was instructing them, in no uncertain terms, to put on their big-boy pants and grow up! God then decided to put Job on the hot seat and ask this blameless man a few questions that resonate with eternal significance.

GOD TALKS. JOB LISTENS.

The writer of the Book of Job devotes two entire chapters, which translates to 67 verses, to the interrogation that God chooses to put Job through. Job is under the light of the grandest inquisition of all time. God questions man. Eternity interrogates the temporary. The divine interviews humanity. Perpetual good examines sin.

"Where were you when I laid the foundation of the earth?

Tell Me, if you have understanding,
Who set its measurements? Since you know,
Or who stretched the line on it?
On what were its bases sunk?
Or who laid its cornerstone,
When the morning stars sang together
And all the sons of God shouted for joy?
Or who enclosed the sea with doors
When, bursting forth, it went out from the womb;
When I made a cloud its garment
And thick darkness its swaddling band,
And I placed boundaries on it
And set a bolt and doors,
And I said, 'Thus far you shall come, but no farther;
And here your proud waves stop?'"—Job 38:4–11

Did you read those eight verses from Job 38? If you skipped over them, go back and read them. God was reminding the man, Job, who God is and what impressive credentials are on His eternal résumé. God reminded the blameless Job that He had been in the authority business since before the world began. So exhaustive and monumental was the account of all that God had created that, at this moment, not only was Job the main captive in God's audience, but all that God had created listened in, as well. The foundation of the Earth paid attention to God's soliloquy of creation, as did the morning stars and the sea. The clouds listened with rapt engrossment, and the oceans stopped their roar as the God of the Universe spoke to the created.

Then the Lord said to Job,
"Will the faultfinder contend with the Almighty?
Let him who reproves God answer it."—Job 40:1–2

I believe that as God was speaking to Job, all of creation

was silent. God's entire creation and the heavenly host who hovered around the throne room of God waited in rapt attention as the God of eternity declared His power to the man of His creative genius. After God finished His impressive speech, which captured the ears of every being in creation, God dared Job to speak. In effect, God was saying, *"Job . . . if you have something to say to Me . . . say it now!"*

Perhaps Job's mouth was dry and his heart was pounding inside the chest that was covered with painful, oozing boils. Perhaps Job hung his head in shame as he considered the influence and care of God Almighty. Did Job stand to his feet in respect as he began to respond to his Creator? Or, like Abram, Moses, and David, did Job bow low in His presence? The Bible does not reveal what the posture of Job was at that moment, but it clearly communicates what was in Job's heart:

Then Job answered the Lord and said,
"Behold, I am insignificant; what can I reply to You?
I lay my hand on my mouth.
Once I have spoken, and I will not answer;
Even twice, and I will add nothing more."—Job 40:3–5

The blameless example of Job echoes through the ages to anyone in any historical junction who encounters the unfairness and the turmoil that wildfires incite. Job humbly but with great esteem recognized that in the presence of God Almighty, a human being truly has nothing to say. Job put his hand over his mouth and stood in the presence of God fully humbled and with no remaining guile.

Job, although alive on the stage of history long before the Solomon the wise, agreed with the royal prudence found in the Book of Ecclesiastes:

Do not be hasty in word or impulsive in thought to bring up a matter in the presence of God. For God is in heaven and you are on the earth; therefore let your words be few.—Ecclesiastes 5:2

Job learned that the only reason for taking your hand off of your mouth in the presence of God is to worship Him. There is no other reason to do so . . . no other reason at all.

God continued to speak with Job in verse after verse and justly reminded this man precisely who God is, all that He has done, and what authority He has possessed since the beginning of all time.

I RETRACT

How does a besieged man respond to a sovereign God? The pure-gold words of Job clearly and beautifully give response to that question:

Then Job answered the Lord and said,
"I know that You can do all things,
And that no purpose of Yours can be thwarted.
'Who is this that hides counsel without knowledge?'
"Therefore I have declared that which I did
not understand,
Things too wonderful for me, which I did not know.
'Hear, now, and I will speak;
I will ask You, and You instruct me.'
"I have heard of You by the hearing of the ear;
But now my eye sees You;
Therefore I retract,
And I repent in dust and ashes."—Job 42:1–6

Perhaps I need to stand humbly beside Job and declare to the Lord, "Therefore I retract." Do you need to join Job and me in that place of self-examination and repentance?

I retract pride and selfishness.

I retract all of the blame that I have spewed on You, God.

I retract insolence and rebellion.

I retract anger and insubordination.

I retract negativity and a critical spirit.

Therefore, I retract, God. I retract.

When the fires of life have done a work so complete and vast in your life that they are able to elicit the response, "Therefore, I retract," it is a beautiful certainty that God has been established upon the throne of the retracted heart. Often, the purpose of the fires of life is lovingly revealed when the one whose life has been impacted by the fire is able to retract and repent.

Job, like Jesus in the Garden of Gethsemane, was able to say, "Not my will, but Your will, O God!" Job was able to confess that he knew that God could do all things and that no purpose of His was able to be thwarted. Job had an "aha!" moment in the presence of His Redeemer and could declare, "I will ask You and You will instruct me." Job's life was in agreement that God was the wise Professor and that Job was the lowly and teachable student.

GOD IS LISTENING

It came about after the Lord had spoken these words to Job, that the Lord said to Eliphaz the Temanite, "My wrath is kindled against you and against your two friends, because you have not spoken of Me what is right as My servant Job has. . . ." So Eliphaz the Temanite and Bildad the Shuhite and Zophar the Naamathite went and did as the Lord told them; and the Lord accepted Job.—Job 42:7, 9

Those words spoken by God to Job's comforters are

sobering verses for those of us who love to give advice and presume to know as much as or more than God. It is vital to remind yourself that Someone is listening to every foolish word spoken and that listener's name is God. Do not falsely believe that it is possible to speak in buffoonery and remain unnoticed by God. The native tongue of the enemy is foolishness or pride; the native tongue of God is wisdom and praise. Which language have you chosen to speak?

FULL OF DAYS!

> *The Lord restored the fortunes of Job when he prayed for his friends, and the Lord increased all that Job had twofold.*—Job 42:10

When Job prayed for the three men who criticized him, blamed him, and mocked his God, the Lord increased everything that Job had before the tragedies. This increase was a double blessing for the man who was blameless and chose to pray for the difficult people in his life. Job did not nurture bitterness, nor did he blame the men who blamed him, but he prayed for them. People can run away from the impact of your words, but they can never escape the power of your prayers. The amazing miracle that happens when a victim chooses to pray rather than retaliate is that the blessing comes back to benefit the one who chose to pray.

When a man or a woman who has been through horrific life circumstances chooses to pray for and bless those who have been the abusers, the Lord will restore the fortunes of the man or woman on their knees. If the Lord did it for Job, He will certainly do it for you! God will restore your reputation and your loss when you choose to pray and not lecture. The Lord will not only restore what you have lost, but He will add His multiplicative touch of the double blessing to your life. The way to access the double blessing in the Kingdom of

God is to pray for the difficult people in your life and keep your life free from blame.

Instead of your shame you will have a double portion, and instead of humiliation they will shout for joy over their portion. Therefore they will possess a double portion in their land, everlasting joy will be theirs.—Isaiah 61:7

The same God who gave to Job a double portion return is the same God whom you serve. The same God who spoke to the prophet Isaiah about the power of a double portion is the same God whom you serve. We serve a God of the double portion who is lavishly generous in blessing His children who choose to pray and worship!

The Lord blessed the latter days of Job more than his beginning; and he had 14,000 sheep and 6,000 camels and 1,000 yoke of oxen and 1,000 female donkeys.—Isaiah 42:12

The first chapter of Job lists the livestock that Job had prior to the very worst day of Job's life: *"His possessions also were 7,000 sheep, 3,000 camels, 500 yoke of oxen, 500 female donkeys . . ."* (Job 1:3). Job was granted exactly double in the number of livestock that he had previously owned. Exactly double!

The worst day of your life is not the end of your story. The worst day of your life is not your legacy. The worst day of your life never determines the goodness of God toward you.

The Lord blessed the latter days of Job more than his beginning, because this is what God does for men and women who declare God's wisdom and power while in the fire. This is what God does for men and women who choose to repent and refuse to blame. This is what God does for men and women who worship while they grieve. Grieve if you must, but do it with your hands in the air! Never allow a season of grief or sorrow to steal the song of joy in your heart.

> *He had seven sons and three daughters. He named the first Jemimah, the second Keziah, and the third Keren-happuch. In all the land no women were found so fair as Job's daughters; and their father gave them inheritance among their brothers. After this, Job lived 140 years, and saw his sons and his grandsons, four generations.*—Job 42:13–16

What a powerful and unusual legacy with which Job, the blameless man, not only blessed his sons but also blessed his beautiful daughters! In a patriarchal society, this was unheard of; women had no more value than did the family cow or sheep. The only redeeming characteristic about women at this time in history was their ability to bear children and to give a man sons in order to carry on the family name. But not for this man, Job! He had learned that every life, man or woman, son or daughter, is a life of dignity and worthy of blessing. When a man or a woman is blameless, their legacy is always one of blessing.

> *And Job died, an old man and full of days.*—Job 42:17

When Job died, he wasn't bitter, but he was a man of blessing! When Job died, he wasn't empty, but he was full! When Job died, he was not filled with pain or regret: Job, the blameless man, was filled with life even on the day of his death. Job's life had not been filled with mere calendar days or the hours ticking by on a clock, but Job's life was filled with the very best things that God can bless a man or a woman with. The fire that violently blew into Job's life had no power over him, because Job, the blameless man, knew the greater power of worship. Job, the greatest man alive, kept his attention and his heart focused on the goodness of God and not upon the temperature of the fire. The Refiner's fire had not only purified this blameless man, but it had ushered in an immeasurable blessing into his life. The Bible describes Job as "full of days" at the end of his life, because the fire had not diminished his ability to live well and to live abundantly. Job, the blameless man, reflected the heart of the blameless God. The fire had enhanced the life of Job because he had chosen to bless God and not blame God.

THE JOY IN THE FIRE

What will you choose to do while in the fire?

Will you bless or will you blame?

Will you whine or will you worship?

How will the Holy Spirit write your obituary?

The legacy of Job can be your legacy, as well! At the end of this journey known as life, regardless of the heat of the fires that you have encountered, let your resounding legacy be that you were a man or a woman who was still abounding with a will to live and a will to worship at the last measured moment of your life. Let your legacy be that the joy of His presence was a far greater and infinitely richer experience than the heat of the fire of life's circumstances that you faced.

There is only one way to survive the fires that you will certainly encounter in the duration of life . . . *make sure that the flame of Christ within you burns far brighter and hotter than any fire that burns around you.* It is with the flame of Christ that you will find the joy in the middle of any ferocious inferno. It is when His presence, which is defined as "joy," becomes your constant and comforting companion, that others will see His reflection in your life. Even in the fire.

ACKNOWLEDGEMENTS

"Refined: Finding Joy In the Midst of the Fire!"

A book is never the reflection of only the author's heart but it is a collection of relationships, events, influencers and teachers over the course of many, many years. And, planted in this author's heart is the garden of so many significant people that it is nearly impossible to count all of the blossoms!

First of all, thank you to my husband, **Craig McLeod,** for loving me . . . for believing in me . . . and for cheering me on!

Thank you to my parents, **Norman and Joan Burton,** who taught me to love the Word of God and who encouraged me to follow resolutely after God.

Thank you to the father that God brought to me later in life, **Leo Ormanoski,** who loves my mother and all of us with a fierce and compassionate love.

Thank you to my in-laws, **Wesley and Becky McLeod,** for raising Craig McLeod to be a man of God and a man of honor.

How I love being the mother to the 5 courageous, unique and delightful McLeod children! Thank you for teaching me how to die to self, how to love extravagantly and how to believe implicitly!

Matthew . . . thank you for being a big brother that the 4 younger McLeod siblings could look up to and admire. Thank you for living for Christ passionately, for dreaming big dreams, for discipling young men on and off the court, and for being a husband and father of love and excellence.

Christopher . . . thank you for being so kind to all of us and for singing the song that you have been given. Thank you for leading 1,000's of people into worship, for writing songs that are touching a generation and for being a husband and father of love and excellence.

Jordan . . . thank you for your laughter and joy through the years. Thank you for teasing us, for encouraging us and for wanting to be with us. Your creativity and talent is unmatched! Pa and Pappy would be so proud of you. Thank you for being a husband and father of love and excellence.

Joy . . . thank you for being a daughter that has grown up to be one of my dearest friends. Thank you for serving God, for serving the church and for serving the world. Thank you for living up to your name and for making a difference in the lives of young women from Texas to NY. I can't wait to see what this year holds for you!

Joni . . . thank you for being such a young woman of determination and virtue. Thank you for serving God and for loving the nations. You are truly a great leader and I know that you are going to change the world! You are always, always in my heart.

And to the incredible 4 young adults that I have gained through marriage!

Emily . . . you are more than a daughter-in-law to me . . . you are a friend and a prayer partner. You are one of the finest women I have ever met . . . and you belong to us!! Thank you for loving Matt, Olivia, Wesley, Boyce and Elizabeth Joy.

Liz . . . what joy it is to watch you love your life! Your compassion and wisdom are truly world-changing in my book! I am so thankful that I get to do life with you! Thank you for loving Christopher, Amelia Grace and Jack Burton.

Allie . . . there are no words to tell you how thankful I am for you, for your heart, for your prayers and for your vision. God has great things for you . . . I don't doubt it for one minute! Thank you for loving Jordan and Ian Wesley.

Chris Barker . . . you are the answer to this mama's prayers! You are a man of valor and of integrity. Thank you for treasuring Joy and for making us feel like the most blessed parents on the face of the planet! Thank you for loving our Joy.

Who knew the absolute delight of grandbabies?!! Keep them coming, McLeod children . . . keep them coming!!

Olivia Mae . . . you are a school-loving, craft-making sweetheart of a girl!

Ian Wesley . . . you are a basketball-playing, joke-telling, brilliant boy!

Wesley Eric . . . you are a ball-playing, book-reading superhero of a boy!

Amelia Grace . . . you are a song-singing, big-dreaming, giggle-creating girl!

Boyce . . . you are an energy-erupting, fun-finding, ball-kicking boy!

Elizabeth Joy . . . you are a sweet-smiling, kissable, much-loved baby girl!

Jack Burton . . . you are a little piece of musical and athletic dynamite just waiting to explode!

And then, I must acknowledge with deep gratitude the dear friends who have become like family to me.

Angela Storm . . . my sister, my friend, my fellow warrior. Thank you for standing in faith with me and for believing in the message of this ministry. Your faithful support has strengthened me in ways that have changed my life.

Monica Orzechowski . . . you truly bring out the best in me! Thank you for your creative genius, for working long hours and for being brave enough to dream with me. You are the little sister that I never had.

Susie Hilchey . . . from the fifth grade until today I am blessed to be your friend. You are a shining example of how God can truly and miraculously change one person's life. You are more like Jesus than anyone I know.

Kim Pickard-Dudley . . . what a gift you are to me and to the ministry! Your spirit of excellence is contagious and you are having a profound impact on more people's lives than you can imagine!

Christy Christopher . . . thank you for your prayers, your encouragement, your insight and your friendship. Our hearts are knit together in love and in ministry. There is no one I would rather have pray for me than you!

Carolyn Hogan . . . my mentor in the faith. Your gentle spirit has sustained me through many a storm. Your wisdom has enriched my life. Because I knew you . . . I have been changed for good.

Shannon Maitre . . . is there anyone more like me on the face of the planet?!! We see eye-to-eye and heart-to-heart on nearly every important issue in life. #therewereneversuchdevotedsisters

Dawn Frink . . . although the years have passed and the times together have been infrequent . . . you are my kindred spirit. Oh! To sit on your front porch with a glass of tea, smelling the lilacs and listening for the song of the birds.

Marilyn Frebersyser . . . every time I drink a cup of tea in a fine china cup, I think of you. Every time I cheer for Duke, I think of you. Every time I want to go out to lunch, I think of you. Every time . . . I think of you.

Kathy Pierce . . . you make me laugh. I keep you stable and you keep me from being boring. I love you completely and thoroughly.

Lynn Parker Fields . . . the La-La of my heart. Our friendship has not diminished over the years but has only grown more precious and valuable. You are my forever friend.

Patricia Apy . . . Isn't it nice to think that tomorrow is a new day with no mistakes in it yet? Which would you rather be if you had the choice . . . divinely beautiful or dazzlingly clever or angelically good? True friends are always together in spirit.

Camella Binkley . . . How rich I am to have you in my life! Your dedication humbles me . . . your generosity challenges me . . . and your wisdom is a gift from the Father. I am blessed to call you friend.

Diane Phelps . . . From little girls who grew up down the street from each other . . . to young mothers who raised their children with passion and resolve . . . to empty-nesters who now find time to go out to dinner and study the Word together. You are a rare and priceless gift, my friend!

And then . . . to the professionals who have cheered for me, advised me and showered me with open doors.

John Mason . . . you will definitely NOT die a copy! There is no one like you . . . you are one of a kind! I am so grateful that you are in my corner.

Chris Busch . . . your thought particles of wisdom and insight are oh! so important to this girl! It's an honor to serve you in ministry and professionally. You are definitely a hall-of-famer in my book!

Scott and Julie Spiewak . . . I am humbled that you would choose to work with me . . . I am honored to call you friends. Let's change the world together!

Peggy and Lloyd Hildebrand . . . Thank you for allowing me to publish the message of my heart. You both are the "real deal" and I respect and admire you greatly.

No More Ordinary
Living the life you were made for

by Carol Burton McLeod

CAROL McLEOD partners with the Word of God and the lives of victorious believers to show you how to obtain and maintain the full and wonderful life that God wants you to have. Your life can be extraordinary!

Learn how to tackle life with zest in spite of the circumstances. Discover how to live the life you were made for, as you learn what made the difference for people like Corrie ten Boom, Robert LeTourneau, Ruth Bell Graham, Hank and Betty Stam, Susannah Wesley, and many others.

The author writes: "This Heaven-guaranteed, extraordinary, too-good-to-be-true life starts the instant a sinner admits his or her need for a Savior. Life with a capital 'L' begins the moment that you make the miraculous decision to enter into a partnership with the Man whose very identity is known as Life himself!"

This book is a no-compromise, how-to-get-there-from-here manual that will take you out of the humdrum and mediocrity of this earthly existence and take you into an abundant life that is full of joy!

CAROL BURTON MCLEOD says, "I am just a girl who is head over heels in love with Jesus. I am passionately addicted to His Word, and I find all the joy I need as I spend time in His presence." She describes herself as a Christmas-holic, and she is very fond of chocolate and enjoys a good read. She doesn't like cleaning her house and has become an expert in carry-out dinners. She hates to shop, loves to jog, and somehow finds time in her busy life to hang out with small children. She is the kind of woman you could laugh with over lunch, cry with over disappointment, and shout over with victory.

ISBN: 978-1-61036-120-0
TPB / 216 pages